"If you drive a car, ride in a car, or wa̶̶̶̶ ̶̶̶ ̶.̶.̶ ̶.̶ ̶̶̶̶̶ where cars drive, this book is a must read. Car insurance advertisements with talking animals may amuse you, but what goes on between insurers and injured people after an auto accident will amaze you."

Insurance Consumer Advocate Amy Bach,
Co-Founder, United Policyholders

"Injured Money is a remarkable book based on the author's first-hand account of a serious accident in which he suffered painful life altering injuries and details his battle with lawyers, doctors and insurance adjusters to recover a very substantial amount of money. Whether you are a legal professional, in the medical field, a first responder, an insurance adjuster, or dealing with a personal injury yourself, this book is an invaluable tool full of insight."

Attorney, Thomas Huppuch

"I only wish this book existed when I had my accident. I probably would not have hired a lawyer and I certainly would have been much better prepared to file my claim and win a larger settlement."

Sandra Kelly, Auto Accident Survivor

"Every person who has insurance should be reading this book. It's not just about showing you step-by-step how to win claims, but it's also about helping you make sure you have partnered with the right insurance company before that fateful accident occurs."

Paul Ferguson, Retired Deputy Sheriff

Injured Money

First Edition 2014

ISBN 978-0-9914391-0-2

Published by Wish to Know
PO Box 10375
Bedford, NH 03110
www.wishtoknow.com

Injured Money™ is a Trademark of Injured Money, LLC
Cover design by Edwar G. Martinez, El Salvador

DISCLAIMER:

This book expresses the author's opinion based on his personal experience which included serious personal injuries, physical and emotional pain, a lengthy recovery, substantial medical bills and hours of dealing with insurance companies, lawyers, adjusters and others. Although the insurance industry, lawyers, adjusters, etc., are maligned in the press and social media, it is the author's opinion that there are honest, hard working and compassionate people and companies out there who can be persuaded to do the right thing when presented with the facts. It is the author's hope this book will be a tool that will help you achieve a better result.

The author does not make any implied or specific warranty or guarantee of any type with regard to the validity of any information contained herein. The information contained herein is provided to assist the reader in determining how to manage a claim or lawsuit against an insurance company. Laws, statutes and procedures change based on the state governing the event, the locality of the event, the insurance company or companies involved and when the event took place.

The author does not advertise, recommend or suggest this book is a substitute for a lawyer, a financial planner or an accountant. For information on specific situations, professional help should be secured.

Table of Contents

Chapter 1 – From the Pavement to "Injured Money"

What started with Emergency Medical Technicians moving my badly injured body from the worn pavement of an intersection into an ambulance concluded with me being awarded more than a quarter of a million dollars from auto insurance companies. What happened in between is a shocking story that every person in America needs to know. The grim reality is that consumers – like you and I – think we are protected because we have insurance. I found out the hard way that this is untrue and wrote "Injured Money" to not only expose how insurance companies behave when claims are filed, but to also help people who have either had an accident or just want to make sure they and their loved ones are protected.

This book is not just about helping someone fight, and win, big insurance claims like I did (and I will show you how to do that) but it's also about helping people choose the right insurance company so that you and your family members are protected when an accident occurs. Looking back, I wish I knew what I know now on that fateful day I was lying on the pavement seriously injured. I am now passing that experience forward to you so that you have the knowledge and the know-how to buy the right insurance today and win big claims in the future in the event that you are involved in an accident.

While writing "Injured Money" took years, the decision to expose the fraudulent action of insurance companies took seconds. From the time I learned my insurance company had modified my medical records, I knew consumers needed to know about the lack of ethics within the insurance industry and how it will personally affect them.

Never in my wildest dreams did I think that my insurance company would lie, twist the truth and even modify my own medical records, making it appear as if my injuries were not a result of the accident. In my view, this is both unethical and unacceptable behavior. To an auto insurance company, I was just another claim they did not want to pay so they could increase their profits.

"Injured Money" is about protecting you and your family with insurance. Whether you read this before or after an accident occurs, this book is a guide to buying and using insurance, and a story about how badly things can go wrong If you don't buy insurance carefully. Key points you will take away from this book include:

- An easy-to-understand guide for winning insurance claims with step-by-step instructions starting from the day you have an accident all the way through winning your claim or lawsuit.
- The "inside story" on how insurance companies operate so that you know what to expect, what to do, and what not to do when dealing with insurance companies who claim they want to 'help you.'
- Advice on how to deal with medical and auto insurance companies when they stop paying your medical bills because they both claim "the other one is responsible. It's no wonder that medical bills are the leading cause of personal bankruptcy in the U.S. In my case, I was faced with $84K of medical bills that no insurance company would pay.
- The know-how to enable you to represent yourself without a lawyer and save significant money on legal fees, as well as recognizing when it's time to hire an attorney to maximize the amount of money recovered.

After writing this book and researching the industry, I discovered how badly the insurance industry needs reform. It is also clear that the new laws under the Affordable Care Act (ObamaCare) do not address the problems with the insurance industry highlighted in this book, making this book a must-read for most Americans.

While this is something of a David and Goliath scenario and people are scared to speak out against Goliath (their insurance company), we are in a new era. In the era of the Internet, we now have nearly 200 million Davids (all consumers like you and I) who can share information to educate each other about insurance companies. For this reason, I have also created the website www.injuredmoney.com to serve as a place where consumers can rate their own insurance companies and share stories about what happened to them. This collection of information will empower consumers to give their business to only the reputable companies who will pay claims on behalf of their policyholders.

The Day That Changes Your Life

For me that day was a sunny Friday morning in June, two days before Father's Day. Our Father's Day plans were for my wife, Kelly, and I to celebrate with our three young children, ages 2, 4 and six weeks old.

It was 8 a.m. and I was enjoying the beautiful morning while riding my bicycle to work. I was a serious cyclist and regularly commuted to work on a bicycle. I always rode the side streets to stay away from heavy traffic.

On this particular morning, a driver coming toward me from the other direction decided – without warning – to abruptly accelerate into a left turn, crossing my path directly in front of me. I was traveling with traffic at 26 mph, giving us a collision speed of approximately 50 mph. The woman speeding through the intersection was watching me every inch of the way. As she steered her car directly at me, she looked over the steering wheel, across the hood, and we locked eyes. She clearly saw me, but did not brake, swerve or take any action to avoid hitting me.

With the quickest reactions I could summon, I swerved toward the middle of the intersection, desperate to avoid a head-on collision. But my reactions had not been quick enough. As I turned, my right hip and chest collided with the passenger side of her car. Upon impact, I flipped up and over her car and landed in the middle of the intersection. She was at fault since I had the right-of-way, but that doesn't help much when you're lying on the pavement seriously injured.

I didn't realize it yet, but my Father's Day plans had suddenly changed. Replacing sleeping-in and playing games in the backyard and swimming in the pool would be Kelly getting a baby sitter to watch the kids in the hospital waiting room, since young children are not allowed into Intensive Care Units (ICU).

At the hospital, it was determined I had broken/displaced ribs, a punctured/collapsed lung and a fractured hip. I was later diagnosed with three slipped vertebrae in my neck. Needless to say, my focus for the next several months was on recovering. I missed ten weeks of work and had significant pain upon returning to my job. My job was also severely impacted as I was expected to continue traveling extensively as I had done before my accident; something that is nearly impossible with neck and hip injuries.

With injuries of this magnitude, the pain lasts for years. As I complete this book, it is over six years later and I still have daily pain as a direct result of the accident.

I found that as the serious pain from one injury began to subside, other injuries would emerge. As an example of this, I did not realize I had injured my neck for several weeks. This was simply a matter of both the pain from more severe injuries (and the narcotics prescribed to manage that pain) masking the pain of less severe injuries.

Note: This is the first important point of the book. When you are injured, it can take days, or even weeks or months, to understand the full scope of your injuries. And, it may take years to figure out to what degree you will recover from the injuries. You need to be careful in your communication with insurance companies until you fully understand the extent of your injuries. Once the insurance claim is filed, adding more injuries that become apparent later (and could have long-term effects despite being less painful initially) gives the insurance company an opportunity to bring into question your credibility. They will try to prove the injuries are not real and that the pain is a figment of your imagination.

So, there I was with a body wracked by injury, a job that was now too difficult to perform and the extra stress these events brought into my family life. As if this was not enough to deal with, the next thing I found out was that my auto insurance company had no intention of helping me in anyway even though I had paid all my bills with them for over 20 years and never made a significant claim.

Following an accident, the last thing a person needs is an insurance company that collects policy dollars but doesn't provide insurance. For this reason, I wrote this book and as you will see in the subsequent chapters, I will use my own personal experiences to walk you through the events immediately following my accident all the way to settling multiple insurance claims and a lawsuit. At every step along the way, you will find a clear description of the pitfalls to avoid so that you too can maximize the money you receive.

Chapter 2 – Immediate Actions Following an Accident

The following chapter outlines the actions you must take immediately after an accident has occurred. These are critical actions so if you are badly injured, you should ask someone you trust to manage them for you. If you do not execute any one of these items, they can, and likely will, significantly reduce the value of your insurance claim.

If you have been in an accident, you likely are wondering if you should hire an attorney. This book will help you make that decision, but start by reading all the way through Chapter 4 first. This is information you need to know, even if you do end up hiring an attorney. If at some point later on you decide that hiring an attorney is best for you, you should then read Chapter 8 so you know how to hire, compensate and manage them.

Beginning with the scene of the accident, we will cover the following five topics:

At the Scene of the Accident

Within Three Days

Communicating with Insurance Companies

Selecting and Communicating with Doctors

Preparation: Enabling You to Win Your Claim

At the Scene of the Accident

To win a Personal Injury (PI) claim from an auto insurance company, you must prove that the other party is responsible (at "fault") for your injuries. Determining the responsible party is obvious in many accidents since roughly half of all accidents involve being rear-ended. In nearly every rear-end accident, fault is assigned to the driver of the car that rear-ended. In cases not involving being rear-ended, fault is assigned to the driver who violated the law, such as ran a red light, made an illegal turn or crossed the center line.

When the responsibility for the accident is not clear, you need to be able to show that it is likely the other party was at fault and caused your injuries. Never admit fault to the other party or witnesses at the scene of the accident. The accident scene is a place where there is an abundance of emotions. The other driver may be yelling at you and accusing you of causing the accident. Be careful not to offer an apology that can later be construed as having admitted fault. A thorough investigation needs to take place to determine fault.

Witnesses

Witnesses to the accident can be very effective at helping you prove fault. Their view of what took place will play a large role in determining who was at fault in the accident. In addition to seeing what took place, witnesses may have heard statements made by the other party, including them admitting fault.

Witnesses can be a stranger, a friend or a relative who saw the accident. Don't hesitate to take an accurate statement from a friend or relative as a witness. Of course, the ideal witness statement is from the other driver admitting fault, but oftentimes the other driver won't admit fault even if they are 100 percent responsible. For any witness, time is of the essence. Get a written and signed statement as soon as possible before they lose interest or their memory begins to fade.

If the written statement is more than one page, have them initial and date each page. Make sure the document includes their contact information so they can be reached later if necessary. See "Appendix C: Accident Details Worksheet" for a form that can help you collect this information. Make sure this Worksheet is filled out in its entirety with name, contact information and details on what happened. Get this form signed by the witness.

To ensure that there is no chance for miscommunication, you should sketch what happened during the accident, showing the roads, which way the cars were traveling, what happened and where the cars ended up. Have all witnesses sign the sketch documenting what happened to indicate they agree with your summary of events as depicted in the sketch.

Other Driver(s)

Make sure to have complete insurance information for the other parties. If there is more than one other driver, get this information from each driver. Do not let another driver sucker you into "privately working it out" between the two of you. This could be a sign they have no insurance, no license, a suspended license or a plan for how to make it appear as if you were at fault.

If another party is driving a borrowed car, you should get insurance information for both the driver and the owner of the vehicle.

Police Report

If you or anyone in your vehicle is injured, or you think there may be injuries involved, call the police so that an official accident report is filed. If you are suffering pain from the accident, make sure the police officer knows this as he may include a mention of this in the accident report. The police officer will investigate what happened by interviewing witnesses, estimating speed by measuring skid marks, diagramming the accident, etc. This information will be used later to determine who was at fault in the accident or if fault for the accident is shared.

In my case, the woman who hit me tried to put the fault of the accident on me by telling the police officer that I was "going too fast." This was obviously absurd since I was on a bicycle and the police officer cited her for not yielding right-of-way. This citation alone proved she was at fault. If you are in a situation where it is not possible to gain agreement on what happened or who is at fault, be sure to make immediate contact with witnesses and call the police so they can investigate. In every case, make sure that as much information as possible is collected at the scene of the accident.

Return to the Scene of the Accident

You should return to the scene of the accident as soon as possible. Visiting the scene of the accident, at around the same time of day, will enable you to identify things that may have contributed to the accident, such as: the angle of the sun, shrubbery hiding a stop sign, or the height of a hill that compromises visibility. Identifying and photographing such items will help you create an accident diagram of what took place and explain what happened.

Checklist of key points learned in this section:

- Witnesses are the best way to prove responsibility for the accident. Get signed statements from them at the scene of the accident or shortly thereafter.
- Get all contact and insurance information at the scene of the accident.
- Never let the other party convince you to "work it out" between the two of you.
- If there are any questions or issues about fault at the scene of the accident, call the police and have them create a report.

To Do:

1. _____

2. _____

3. _____

4. _____

At the Scene of the Accident – Immediate Actions

Print this page and keep it in your glove box so you know what to do at the scene of an accident.

If Injuries

- Call the police.
- Seek medical help within 24 hours.

Information to Collect

- Get signed statements from witnesses stating what they saw.
- Get insurance and contact information for all drivers.
- Get vehicle information (make, model, license plate #) for all vehicles.

Other Actions

- Do not admit fault.
- Do not let other drivers convince you to "work it out." Get their contact and insurance information.

Keep Reading to Understand the Following Points

- Do not speak with the other party's insurance company.
- Do not admit fault to your own insurance company.

Within Three Days of the Accident

The actions you need to take within three days of the accident are identified in this section.

See a Doctor

Injuries need to be attended to by a doctor, clinic or hospital within 24 hours. If you wait longer, the injuries will be viewed as not being severe enough to merit compensation by the insurance company. When having the injuries checked out, make sure you point out all the complaints or areas where you are having pain. Even if you feel only minor pain, report it to the doctor. The minor pain may become significant in a day or a week. It is imperative that all injuries are listed in the initial medical report.

File an Accident Report with the DMV

If a police report was not made at the time of the accident and there is property damage (many states have a threshold of $500 or greater) or there are injuries, you need to file a report with the Department of Motor Vehicles (DMV). In most states, an accident report must be filed with the DMV within 72 hours.

The DMV for your state will likely have a specific form to use when filing an accident report. Be certain to use the correct form. The forms should be available to download from their website. When filling out the report, you should stick to the facts and do not admit that you were responsible (at fault), careless or negligent in any way. It is important that every injury be listed, but you do not need to comment on the severity of the injuries. When in doubt, list them, all of them. If you have a report from a doctor, emergency room, or Emergency Medical Technician (EMT) regarding your injuries, you can quote directly from that report.

Notify Your Insurance Company

You should let your insurance company know about the accident and injuries as soon as possible. The insurance policy documentation will state how much time is allowed to report an accident. If you don't have this, call the insurance company and ask them. You should be careful about what you say and you should not admit fault. While your list of injuries needs to be complete, you should not elaborate. If ever in doubt, just say "no comment" or "I'm not prepared to talk about that right now."

If you purchased the insurance coverage through an insurance agent, someone who sells insurance on behalf of the insurance company, then you should contact your agent to file the report. There are many benefits to working with the agent versus directly with the insurance company. Most likely, you have some level of personal relationship with your agent and they understand the insurance policy in detail. They will be able to identify the types of coverage for which you qualify, ensuring you get the maximum benefit allowed under the policy. For example, in a property damage claim on a damaged car, the agent can explain the coverage for getting your car towed, for renting another car, what type of car you can get, for how long, how it will be paid for and other details.

If you purchased insurance online or over the phone, you should go through the website or to their customer support line to file the report. You will need to ask specific questions about the additional benefits of the insurance policy such as a rental car or towing of your damaged vehicle. Unlike agents, employees in call centers are sometimes trained not to highlight these benefits for you, or may not have visibility to what benefits your policy provides.

If you don't hear back from your agent or insurance company with a claim number within one week, you should follow-up to make sure a claim number has been assigned. Once the claim number is assigned, you should make sure that all documentation you submit in the future has this claim number in the header or footer of each page of documentation related to your claim.

If you don't have an agent, you will need to notify your insurance company directly. Being careful what you tell them still applies.

Notify All Parties

You need to notify all parties involved in the accident. The following is an example list of who should be notified:

- Insurance claims departments of all drivers.
- In the event someone was the driver of a borrowed or company owned vehicle, also notify the insurance claims department of the vehicle owner.
- Employers of drivers for any vehicle used for company business.
- Any person who may have contributed to the accident such as leaving an obstruction in the roadway.

The notification you send to each party should be a short letter stating the date, time and location of the accident and identification of the people and vehicles involved. If an employer is involved, you should notify the employer and ask them for their insurance company information if you do not have this yet. An example letter follows below.

Letter 1: Sample letter of notification.

Today's Date

Your Name
Address

Insurance company name or employer name
Address

Re: Name of person involved in accident (their insured or their employee)

Dear: "insurance company name" or "employer name"

At "time" on "date" at "location of accident" an accident occurred involving "names of all parties and the vehicle they were driving (make, model, color and license plate number).

Regards,

First name, last name

The notification letter should not include any details such as who is at fault, the physical damage, injuries sustained or the claims you intend to file. Once you have notified all the parties involved of your intent to file a claim, the insurance companies will want to speak with you, hoping to get statements that compromise your claim. The following section describes how to manage your communication with insurance companies.

Checklist of key points learned in this section:

- To have a legitimate bodily injury claim, you will need to seek professional medical help within 24 hours of the accident.
- If there is property damage or injuries involved, you must file an accident report with the DMV (or equivalent) in your state.
- You need to file an accident report with your insurance company. If you have an agent, do it through the agent and ask the agent about all the coverage you have that applies to your accident.
- In accident reports do not admit fault, do give a complete list of all known injuries, but do not elaborate. Just provide the facts.
- You do not need to file an accident report with the other party's insurance company but you should notify all insurance companies of the accident.

To Do:

1. _____

2. _____

3. _____

4. _____

5. _____

Communicating with Insurance Companies

Once the insurance companies are aware of the accident, they will begin collecting information about the accident and your injuries. You will get requests from both your own insurance company and the other party's insurance company. These requests will include phone calls directly to you, as well as by mail. When they call, they will try to get information from you or whoever answers the phone.

You must be very careful about what you say. The insurance company representatives are trained to sound as if they truly care about you, but they are really just trying to get information that will ultimately help the insurance company reduce the amount of money you will receive. If in doubt on what to say when they call, you should just say "I'm not prepared to talk about that at the moment. I need to first collect all the facts about the accident and complete my treatment by doctors." They will not give up so you will need to be prepared to repeat yourself. Be firm, but be polite.

The Claims Adjuster's (Representative's) Role

The "claims adjuster" historically was the person who understood the claim in great detail and determined the value of the claim in order to properly compensate the person making the claim. Over the last couple of decades, this role has been taken over by computers. The claims adjuster is now often referred to as the "insurance company representative" since the job doesn't include "adjusting" any longer. This will be your primary point of contact at the insurance company.

The insurance company representative's role is to be a liaison and has little to do with determining the value of your claim. Their job is to gain your trust. Once trust is gained, the insurance company is in a position to delay the processing of your claim and potentially deny your claim. Ultimately, you may be put in a position where you no longer have an option to file a lawsuit because they delayed long enough that you ran out of time.

The methods they will use to get information from you will include calling you at home or at work (anywhere they can get someone on the phone). They will engage you (or whoever answers the phone) in a conversation, asking questions about how you are doing, the nature of the injuries, the treatment you have received and your recovery process. They are trained to present a case to you that they are doing this out of concern for you and for your protection. This is not true. In reality, they are looking for information or statements from you that will minimize their payment to you.

They may ask you if they can take a recorded statement. While they will tell you this statement is to protect you in the future, they are really looking to get a statement from you that includes an incomplete or incorrect description of the injuries, or that the injuries are healing (that may be true now, but could change at any time). Make sure anyone who answers your phone (spouse, children, assistant, etc.) knows not to give them any information.

The insurance company will also send you forms to sign that authorize the release of medical information to them. This is known as a "release form" or some similar name. They will continue to send these forms to you regularly for countless months, hoping that at some point you will sign the form and send it back. They may also ask you to visit their own physicians to get a second opinion. How you handle these forms and physician requests depends on who sent them to you. The following describes how to handle these requests from both the other party's insurance company and your own.

The Other Party's Insurance Company

If you were injured and the other party was at fault, either partially or wholly, in the accident, then their insurance company owes you compensation (money). Since you do not have a contract with the other party's insurance company, you are not obligated to provide them any information. The only information they will have is from the police report and whatever their insured has told them. To get more information, they will aggressively pursue you and if you provide any inaccurate or incomplete information, they will use this against you later on.

Never give any information such as verbal or recorded statements, medical records or work records to an insurance company other than your own. You can simply tell them you are not prepared to give a statement at this time. If you feel you must say something, simply repeat the information that was provided in the written notification (date, time and location of the accident, and identification of the people and vehicles involved) you sent to all parties. Do not give any additional information. Also, never sign a form releasing any medical information to them or visit their doctor.

Your Insurance Company

Since you have a contract in place with your own insurance company, this contract requires you to share medical and work records with them in order to file a claim. This can be done in two ways:

- The recommended approach is for you to get copies of all your hospital, medical, and doctor's records and send them to the insurance company.

The Reason for Waiting to Share Information

The passage of time brings clarity to any situation. Examples could be an injury involving brain damage, or a homeowner's insurance claim for fire damage. In serious situations like these, the insurance company will work aggressively to "help you" by settling quickly. Keep in mind that if the insurance company wants to settle quickly, this probably means they think you have a good case. They know that if they settle quickly, you can't come back for more money later on when you discover other injuries or property damage that was not initially evident.

Whether you are providing information about injuries to your own (or another) insurance company, you should take the time needed until your injuries are fully understood and then provide the information necessary to document the injuries. The reason for waiting is that the recovery process is a long and winding road. One day you may feel like you are making great progress, then suddenly there is a setback and the outcome doesn't look so rosy. An example of how this could work against you is as follows: You had surgery that went well, the sutures were removed, the inflammation went down and now you are starting therapy. So far everything has gone perfectly. From here it would be easy to project that you will be fully recovered in 10 weeks (as an example). But in reality, the surgery didn't repair everything and there will be a long-term limitation you have not yet identified.

During the period of time where everything is going well, you may report to the claims representative that everything is going well and that you expect to be fully recovered in 10 weeks. One or two years later when you complain of lingering pain and limited function, they will refer to this statement you gave them and claim that you are now faking it in order to maximize the value of the case. Don't give them a tool like this to use against you.

Quick Guide to Handling Claims Representatives

In summary, the following guidelines will prevent you from giving insurance companies information to use against you:

The Other Party's Insurance Company

- Give no information.
- Never allow them to take a recorded message.
- Do not sign any documents from the other party's insurance company.

Your Own Insurance Company

- Provide only the facts and do not elaborate.
- Provide all medical records yourself.
- If you grant the insurance company direct access to doctors and hospitals for collecting medical records, limit their access to the timeframe relevant to the accident.
- If you get second opinions on injuries, do not give names of doctors you saw that had a differing opinion of your injuries.
- Be consistent in the information you provide.
- Do not get trapped into long conversations.
- When pressed for information or when in doubt, say that you are not prepared to talk at this time and have no comment.

Both Insurance Companies

- Be suspicious if they are pushing for a quick settlement.
- Make sure other people who may answer your phone or mail give no information on your behalf.
- Keep detailed notes of every conversation.

Checklist of key points learned in this section:

- Prepare your family, or people who answer your phone at work, not to give any information to the insurance company if they call.

- If an insurance company wants to settle a claim quickly, be suspicious. They are trying to limit their liability or get you to accept a low-ball offer (or both).

- Limit the medical records shared with the insurance company to records relevant to the accident. The best way to do this is for you to take control and collect all the records, review them and provide them to the insurance company.

- Check with the insurance company to make sure providing the records to them, rather than them collecting the records from the doctors and hospital themselves, is okay. If so, have them make a note in your file that they approved this. They will want to collect the records themselves since this gives them a better chance of getting information that may be harmful to you.

- Wait to provide a complete set of records once injuries are fully understood.

- Keep detailed notes of every conversation with any person representing an insurance company. Forms are available in Appendix D.

To Do:

1. _____

2. _____

3. _____

4. _____

5. _____

6. _____

Selecting and Communicating with Doctors

Once you are beyond the emergency room, you can start having input on the medical staff that treats you. Once you are out of the hospital, the choice of physicians is entirely up to you. The doctor you select may be a doctor you already know and others are likely to be specialists you've never heard of before. When you are making the selection process for these doctors, there are three important factors to keep in mind:

- Get the best doctor available.
- Be careful of what you say. Any information you provide may go in the medical record and will be reviewed later by the insurance company.
- Get a doctor who will offer an opinion, not simply a report.

Get the Best Doctor Available

Finding a good doctor is not easy. Nearly everyone will recommend their doctor unless the doctor totally botched a diagnosis, surgery or treatment. Ask your friends and relatives for referrals and research doctors online.

Don't just rely on the advice of laymen in making your selection. For a more thorough selection process, you should ask other doctors who the local and regional experts are for the needed treatment. In the case of my hip, the doctor assigned to me in the hospital, who was highly regarded in his own right, recommended me to another hip doctor who had more experience. In fact, he had taught the hospital assigned doctor and had done the type of hip surgery I needed more than anyone else in the field. I went with the more experienced doctor.

Be Careful of What You Say

Statements you make during routine office visits will go in your medical record and will be reviewed later by the insurance company. You should not tell untruths about your plight, but don't be like me. When I am injured, it becomes a challenge to see how quickly I can recover and I want to make sure the doctor knows I am setting a record for a quick recovery. But, I've found it's not possible to defy the laws of nature and no matter how many times you say you're doing great, you still don't recover any faster. And the harder you push, eventually you will have a setback. However, the insurance company will not be shy about quoting your records saying how well you said you were doing.

Get a Doctor with an "Opinion"

Whenever possible, you should get a doctor who will offer an "opinion" and not simply a report. A report describes what the doctor did and what was seen, but that isn't all encompassing. For example, before the accident, my hip wasn't perfect and while I had a limited range of motion, it didn't bother me. In fact, I didn't even know I had a limited range of motion until doctors told me. I also learned that loss of range-of-motion is common in people who exercise a lot, which I did. It is a result of an increase in bone mass in weight bearing regions such as hips.

It turns out that the hip specialist I was assigned to at the hospital would not offer a medical opinion because the hospital had a policy against offering opinions. If he had done my hip surgery and was deposed by my insurance company, his statements would have just included the facts and he would not have given an opinion about my expected condition in five, ten or twenty years. Had the insurance company deposed this doctor, his lack of an opinion may have resulted in their winning the argument that my hip would have needed replacement in the future due to my pre-existing condition of limited range-of-motion. This could have had the impact of significantly devaluing my personal injury claim from the accident.

Fortunately for me, I decided not to use the doctor assigned to me at the hospital and instead hired a hip doctor who was a leader and innovator in his field AND was not afraid of offering a medical opinion. When this doctor was asked during a deposition whether I "will ever need my hip replaced as a result of the accident" my doctor answered, "He probably will." In support of this opinion, the doctor went on to describe the problem in my hip as a direct result of the accident.

Despite all the other events you will read about in this book, the words "he probably will" may have been the three words that turned the claim in my favor. I was fortunate to have a doctor who would offer an opinion.

The Medical Report

Before filing an insurance claim, you will need a medical report from your doctor that will likely include a combination of facts and opinions. This may be one report or in the case of multiple injuries, include a collection of reports. These reports will be a key element for determining the compensation you are due and should include the following items:

- How long were you disabled? This is measured as being unable to perform your work and activities of daily living.
- Was your disability total or partial?
- Was the disability directly and solely a result of the accident?
- If there were pre-existing conditions that made your condition worse, work with the doctor to word these carefully.
- What treatments were given?
- What medications were prescribed and for how long?
- What is the future outlook of your disability or pain and how much of this can be directly attributed to the accident?

Checklist of key points learned in this section:

- Ask your current doctor from whom he recommends getting a second opinion.
- Check online to find the names of other specialists in your region. If there are well known specialists outside the region, call them and ask them who is the expert in your local area.
- Before each doctor's appointment, think about what you are going to say to your doctor and how you will say it. If there are specific things about your condition that you want captured in the medical records, ask the doctor to include a statement in the notes.
- Ask your doctor if he were deposed whether he would provide a medical opinion or only a medical report?

To Do:

1. _____

2. _____

3. _____

4. _____

Preparation: Enabling You to Win Your Claim

Now is the time to start preparing your personal injury claim for the auto insurance company. This claim is your demand for financial recovery compensating you for losses following an accident. The preparation for a claim is the same whether you file the claim with your own insurance company, the other party's insurance company or even if you end up hiring an attorney.

The information for your claim needs to be organized and you need to make sure a complete set of documentation exists. To do this, you should get an expanding file from a local office supply store and create sections for:

- Medical bills – create a summary of the medical bills as they arrive. See "Appendix E: Medical Bills" for how to create this summary and what information is required.
- Doctors' reports.
- Accident report and witness statements. See "Appendix C: Accident Details Worksheet" for the forms to fill out.
- Written communication to/from the other party's insurance company.
- Written communication to/from your insurance company.
- Photos from the scene of the accident, of your injuries, etc.

As copies of bills or letters from insurance companies arrive, you should immediately put them in this file folder. This way you know where everything is located and it will be easy to calculate the value of the claim and create the package of information you need to submit with the claim. Even if you end up hiring an attorney, all of this information will still be necessary.

There will also be information you must create. Examples of this information include:

- Notes from conversations with insurance companies (both yours and the other party's) – see "Appendix D: Insurance Information."
- Pictures of injuries and damaged property.
- Anything else you feel may be useful.

You will want notes about what happened before, during and after the accident, including how you felt, how you feel now, the injuries you have and anything else you feel is relevant. It is imperative that you begin taking these notes immediately. With the rush of emotions and flurry of activity following an accident, the memories will soon fade. Capturing emotions and memories on paper will enable you to come back to that moment in time and explain to others what happened in clear and vivid detail.

Take and keep photos of anything relevant, including damage to automobiles or personal property, skid marks, injuries, bruises or incisions from surgery, the bottles of prescribed pain medication, even photos of the bloody clothing they cut off you at the scene of the accident. Photographs are a good way of proving the injuries were real when the insurance company's lawyer questions the validity of your injuries at a future date. Photos show drama in a way words cannot describe.

If you know that you do not want to represent yourself, or you think you need help building your case, you should consider contacting an attorney quickly after the accident. Just remember that you don't have to a sign a contract with an attorney immediately even though an attorney will try to get you to sign quickly if you have a strong claim. The benefit of contacting an attorney early is that he can help determine if you have collected the right evidence to prove fault and provide helpful information on filing a claim. Keep in mind that even if you contact an attorney quickly, you will still need to take the actions in this section and you will need the guidance provided throughout the book. Before signing any agreement with an attorney to represent you, read Chapter 8 on hiring, compensating and managing an attorney.

Checklist of key points learned in this section:

- Take photos of injuries and any damage related to your claim.
- Get organized!

To Do:

1. _____

2. _____

3. _____

Chapter 3 – How to Avoid Losing Medical Coverage

Liability following an accident is based on who is at fault or responsible for the accident. Under normal conditions, your medical insurer has responsibility for covering medical bills. After an auto accident, the auto insurance company of the party at fault becomes responsible. This change in who's responsible following an accident has the potential to leave you without medical coverage because your health insurance company is not responsible, but the auto insurer does not want to accept responsibility. This chapter covers what to do to avoid suffering a gap in medical coverage, a problem that can be financially and medically devastating.

Who is Financially Responsible?

When you are involved in an automobile accident, the automobile insurance of the party at fault becomes liable for covering medical expenses. The auto insurance company of the party at fault is liable for the amount up to the limit, or maximum, of the auto policy. If the party at fault does not have insurance, then your own auto insurance takes over the responsibility as long as you have Uninsured Motorist (UM) coverage as part of your policy. In either of these situations, your medical insurance provider is no longer liable for your medical bills.

The possibility of not being responsible for medical expenses is the reason your medical insurance company wants to determine whether your medical expenses were related to an automobile accident, and what insurance coverage was in place at the time of the accident. To avoid falling into the situation where both the medical insurance and the auto insurance company refuse to pay your medical bills, you need to work with the medical insurance company to ensure continued coverage. The following two sections describe how to work through this situation.

Before Your Medical Insurer Calls

When you are injured, your medical bills immediately become numerous and large. Your medical insurance provider will quickly notice this and will call to determine if you were in an auto accident, and if so, which automobile insurance companies were involved. Before you receive this call, you should understand how your medical insurer handles accidents and whether an auto insurance company becomes liable for the medical bills. You can find this information by reading the medical insurance company's policy handbook, or (if your medical insurance is through your employer) contact your company's Human Resource department.

When Your Medical Insurer Calls

Plan on getting a call from your medical insurance company to determine if you were involved in an accident involving an automobile as soon as the medical bills begin to arrive at your insurance company. Unusually large bills, or items such as an ambulance ride and a hospital visit will trigger them to either call directly or contact you by mail with a questionnaire.

Whether contacted by mail or via the telephone, the medical insurance company is going to want to know the following:

- Were you involved in an automobile accident?
- Who was at fault?
- Which automobile insurance companies are representing the vehicles and people involved?
- What is the medical coverage of the policies?
- Are you planning to file a Personal Injury claim?

The first question about whether you were involved in an automobile accident must be answered with complete accuracy. Trying to hide that you were in an accident involving a motor vehicle could have serious repercussions, including cancellation of your medical insurance.

Questions two through four are questions you need to know. If you don't know the answer, start working to find out. On question five (whether you are planning to file a Personal Injury claim), honesty is the best policy. If you are uncertain as to what degree you will prosecute a damages claim, then you can honestly say you do not yet know. If you definitely plan to file a claim, then you should state this. However, the downside of letting the medical insurance company know your intentions is that when they find out your plans, they may not want to continue paying your medical bills.

When you speak with your medical insurance company, you should ask them if there are any actions you must take to ensure continued medical coverage. Some medical insurance companies have a form commonly referred to as a 'third-party-liability form.' This form states that they will continue paying your medical bills as long as you pay them back in the event you settle a claim with an auto insurance company.

Before signing this 'third-party-liability' form, you should make sure the following three clauses are included:

- You only reimburse them if there is a settlement with the party that is liable.
- You only reimburse them for the amount they paid to your doctor, hospital and other medical

Chapter 4 – What's Your Claim Worth?

After completing this chapter and determining the potential value of your claim, you will know whether pursuing the claim is worth your time and effort. The steps outlined in this chapter are best started once your physical recovery is well underway. In fact, it is necessary to wait until you have an accurate estimate of the total medical costs and time missed at work before you can estimate the claim value. As you improve physically, you will be able to better determine whether you will recover fully, or if there will be lingering issues and limitations, both of which impact the value of the claim.

Following is a short description of each of the four sections contained within this chapter:

Valuing Your Claim

Knowing whether to pursue an insurance claim starts with knowing the value of the claim. How to value a bodily injury claim is covered in detail in the section titled "Valuing Your Claim."

Could I Lose Money on a PI Claim?

Many accident victims worry that filing a PI claim could lead to financial loss. The section titled "Could I Lose Money on a PI Claim" covers what to do to ensure you do not lose money on your claim.

Legal Review

The section titled "Legal Review" explains how to get input on whether there are special circumstances you need to be aware of with regards to your claim. The actions identified in this section will also help you start building a list of attorneys you may want to contact at a later date.

Is the Claim Worth Filing?

Whether the claim is worth filing is the most important nugget of information. This section shows you how to estimate the financial recovery you can expect to receive so you can make this important decision.

Valuing Your Claim

Insurance companies handle property damage claims, such as damage to vehicles, houses or other personal property, and PI claims, such as a hurt back or broken leg, separately. For this reason, the focus of this section is on valuing PI claims. Property damage claims are much more straightforward to value and are addressed separately in Appendix B.

Valuing a PI claim is a process of estimating what a jury might award you if your case went to court. The factors involved in making this estimate are partially measurable, such as the total cost of medical bills and lost income. However, valuing the claim is also largely subjective because it includes items such as how much you have suffered and will continue to suffer. If the case goes to a jury trial, subjective factors such as whether you are a likable person who evokes sympathy, is also an important factor.

To learn the value range of your claim without going through the math, use the claim calculator on the Injured Money website at www.injuredmoney.com. Once at the website, navigate to the Claim Calculator and follow the instructions. This calculator will give you the minimum and maximum value of your claim. To understand this value range more thoroughly, follow the description below.

To understand claim value, let's start by reviewing the measurable items of medical bills and lost income to establish a claim value. The formula for establishing the value of your claim is as follows:

CLAIM VALUE = ((PAIN & SUFFERING + LOST INCOME + LOST
     OPPORTUNITY) X (OTHER PARTY'S % OF FAULT)) – MEDICAL LIENS

Don't worry; this is not nearly as complicated as it looks. The following breaks down the equation into each section and demonstrates how to calculate the claim value.

Pain and Suffering

CLAIM VALUE = ((**PAIN & SUFFERING** + LOST INCOME + LOST
     OPPORTUNITY) X (OTHER PARTY'S % OF FAULT)) – MEDICAL LIENS

To calculate pain and suffering, you must know the sum of your medical bills and multiply that total dollar amount by a "multiplier" between 2 and 10. This multiplier is determined by the severity of the injuries. The more severe and disabling your injuries, the larger the multiplier used to calculate pain and suffering will be.

The total amount of the medical bills is commonly referred to as "medical special damages." Don't be concerned with this term that sounds both technical and nonsensical. This is simply a lawyer's way of saying "total medical bills." Examples of medical expenses that are included in the total medical bills are:

- Ambulance services
- Hospital, clinic or emergency room
- Medical doctors
- Tests such as, X-Rays, MRIs, CT-Scan, etc.
- Laboratory fees
- Medication (prescription and over the counter)
- Medical equipment such as crutches, wheelchair, walker, bandages, etc.
- Physical therapy
- Nursing care
- Transportation to and from medical appointments

To help explain how to calculate pain and suffering, I will use two real-life examples. The first example, which is shown in Table 1, involves a "Serious Injury" and the second example in Table 3 involves a "Minor Injury."

Table 1 below outlines the medical bills accumulated in our "Serious Injury" example. The "Invoice Amount" is the amount billed by the medical provider, while the "Insurance Paid Amount" is how much the medical insurance actually paid. The medical insurance company never pays the full amount billed by the doctor, hospital, or medical provider. While the doctor bills an "Invoice Amount," the medical insurance company pays only a pre-negotiated amount, which is always less than the invoiced amount. Thus, when totaling the medical bills, always include the "Invoice Amount" billed by the provider, not the amount actually paid by the medical insurance company.

Table 1: Example Medical Bills for the Serious Injury Example.

	Invoice Amount	Insurance Paid Amount	Deductible Amount	Description	Service Date	Hospital / Dr. Name
	$1,500.00	$900.00	$100.00	Ambulance	Jan. 2	Ambulance Co.
	$100.00	$60.00	$10.00	X-ray	Jan. 2	Hosp. XYZ
	$2,500.00	$1,500.00	$250.00	Emerg. Rm	Jan. 2	Hosp. XYZ
	$8,000.00	$4,500.00	$400.00	Surgery	Jan. 3	Dr. QRS
	$5,500.00	$3,000.00	$255.00	Hospital	Jan. 3	Hosp. XYZ
	$1,250.00	$650.00	$100.00	Anesthesiologist	Jan. 3	Dr. BZD
	$100.00	$60.00	$10.00	X-ray	Jan. 3	Hosp. XYZ
	$475.00	$200.00	$100.00	Med. Supplies	Jan. 3	Hosp. XYZ
	$1,200.00	$600.00	$60.00	Therapy	Jan. 5	Clinic QRS
Total	$20,625.00	$11,470.00	$1,285.00			

In Table 1 above, the total Invoice Amount is $20,625 for the Serious Injury example. For this Serious Injury example, let's assume surgery and two years of rehabilitation is required for the full recovery of an injured joint, but there will be no permanent consequence. In this case, the range for the pain and suffering multiplier from Table 2 below would be three to five. We will select the middle of the range, using four (4) as our multiplier.

Table 2: Pain and Suffering Multipliers.

Severity	Time to Recover	Multiplier
Non-permanent injury	Less than one year	2 to 3
Non-permanent injury	Two to three years	3 to 5
Permanently disabling	Never	5 to 10
Permanent injury, seriously disabling	Never	10+

Thus, to calculate the pain and suffering amount for this serious injury, we simply multiply $20,625 (the total medical bills from Table 1) x 4 (the middle of the range for the pain and suffering multiplier from Table 2). The resulting pain and suffering for this serious injury would be $82,500.

PAIN AND SUFFERING (SERIOUS INJURY EXAMPLE) = $20,625 X 4
   = $82,500

We will now use the same approach to show how to calculate pain and suffering in a "Minor Injury" example. In this scenario, let's say the person injured the same joint, but only required therapy and would be fully recovered within one year. The medical bills for this injury are outlined in Table 3 below:

Table 3: Example Medical Bills with "Minor Injuries" Claim
        Example.

	Invoice Amount	Insurance Paid Amount	Deductible Amount	Description	Service Date	Hospital / Dr. Name
	$1,500.00	$900.00	$100.00	Ambulance	Jan. 2	Ambulance Co.
	$100.00	$60.00	$10.00	X-ray	Jan. 2	Hosp. XYZ
	$2,500.00	$1,500.00	$250.00	Emerg. Rm	Jan. 2	Hosp. XYZ
	$475.00	$200.00	$60.00	Med. Supplies	Jan. 3	Hosp. XYZ
	$1,200.00	$600.00	$60.00	Therapy	Jan. 5	Clinic QRS
Total	$5,775.00	$3,260.00	$480.00			

In this case, the total Invoice Amount of the medical bills was $5,775. Since the recovery time for this Minor Injury would be less than one year, the range for the multiplier from Table 2 would be two to three. We will use three (3), yielding a pain and suffering amount of $5,775 X 3 = $17,325.

PAIN AND SUFFERING (MINOR INJURY EXAMPLE) = $5,775 X 3
   = $17,325

The multipliers and descriptions included in Table 2 are for common injuries frequently experienced in accidents. For more severe injuries such as spinal cord injuries, brain damage or lost limbs, the pain and suffering amount could be much higher. For cases with severe injuries, professional legal counsel is recommended. In these situations, pay special attention to chapter 8 on hiring, compensating and managing an attorney.

With any injury, and particularly in the case of severe injuries, you should not let the auto insurance company rush you into a settlement. If you have a good case, the insurance company will try to settle quickly before you understand the full extent or ramifications of your injuries, or have the opportunity to find legal counsel that can help you assess the full value of your injuries.

Lost Income

CLAIM VALUE = ((PAIN & SUFFERING + **LOST INCOME** + LOST OPPORTUNITY) X (OTHER PARTY'S % OF FAULT)) – MEDICAL LIENS

Now let's calculate the next item in the equation, lost income. Lost income includes the total amount of income (before taxes are withheld) that you did not receive as well as vacation time and sick time taken from your job as a direct result of the accident. This can easily be shown with documentation that shows the amount of time you missed at work and what you would have earned during that time. An example of this calculation follows: You work an eight-hour day, get paid $50 per hour and missed five days of work. The calculation for lost income would be:

LOST INCOME = 8 HRS/DAY X $50/HR X 5 DAYS = $2,000.

Whatever the amount of lost income, it does not matter if you took the time off without pay, took vacation time, or took medical leave. In all cases, you lost the use of the vacation time or sick leave. The party responsible for the accident must compensate you for that loss.

To prove lost income, you will need a letter signed by someone at your company documenting the time you were away from work and what that time represents in gross, or pre-tax compensation. This letter would likely come from the HR or payroll department.

If you work part-time or are self-employed, you can use the prior year's W2 to show your annual income divided by 52 (weeks in the year) to show your average weekly income. This can be used to estimate your income on a weekly basis.

Commissions and overtime pay can also be estimated in the same way as income for part-time or self-employed work. You simply need to identify the overtime and commission portion of the prior year's W2, divide that by 52 and use this as a weekly estimate. If you work for tips and gratuities, your employer should be able to help you document the lost income you would have expected to receive from tips and gratuities.

For a stay-at-home mom or dad, the rate of pay you can justify for domestic work is equivalent to what it would cost to hire someone to come in and complete the work. Contact an agency to get quotes to determine the cost of such services.

In these examples, Lost Income for both the Serious Injuries and Minor Injuries is the same. Completing the lost income calculation for each example yields the following:

LOST INCOME = 8 X $50 X 5 = $2,000

Lost Opportunity

CLAIM VALUE = ((PAIN & SUFFERING + LOST INCOME + **LOST OPPORTUNITY**) X (OTHER PARTY'S % OF FAULT)) – MEDICAL LIENS

Now it's time to determine if you have lost opportunities to add to the value of your claim. A lost business opportunity is money you may have earned if you were not injured. Lost opportunities are more difficult to prove than lost income, but nevertheless can strengthen your claim by demonstrating the significant impact the accident had on your life. Even if you cannot prove lost opportunity convincingly, it can help strengthen your claim. For example, if you are a contractor and you had to turn business away until you recovered, you could show the value of that business and the income you could have generated.

The challenge in proving lost opportunity is proving the opportunity was real. Having a signed contract, letter of intent, customer feedback on a quotation you provided or a schedule for the work that was supposed to be done are all items you can use to help prove the opportunity was real.

Fault

CLAIM VALUE = ((PAIN & SUFFERING + LOST INCOME + LOST
      OPPORTUNITY) X (**OTHER PARTY'S % OF FAULT**)) – MEDICAL LIENS

Fault is the responsibility for the accident. If some of the responsibility for the accident is attributed to you, this will directly reduce the value of your claim. If the police filed an accident report, they will assign fault in the report. If there is no police report, you will need to establish fault in the negotiations with the insurance company.

Insurance policies only pay you when the other party is at fault. This means, if you were 100% at fault (meaning you caused the accident), the value of the claim to you is $0. Conversely, if the other party is 100% at fault, you collect the full settlement amount. In the case where fault is shared, the value of your claim is reduced by your percentage of the fault. Total fault always equals 100%. To calculate the other party's percentage of fault you need to start with total fault (100%) and subtract your percentage of fault. Using an assumption that you are 20% at fault, let's calculate the other party's percentage of fault. The equation is Total fault – your fault = other party's fault.

OTHER PARTIES % OF FAULT = 100% - 20% = 80%

Many accidents involve one driver rear-ending another. In almost every case the driver who rear ends the other is at fault.

Medical Liens

CLAIM VALUE = ((PAIN & SUFFERING + LOST INCOME + LOST
     OPPORTUNITY) X (OTHER PARTY'S % OF FAULT)) – **MEDICAL LIENS**

A medical lien is the legal right of a medical insurance company to be reimbursed the money they paid for treatment you needed as a result of the accident. The medical insurer has this right based on the responsibility for medical care being transferred to the party at fault when the accident occurred (as discussed in Chapter 3). What this means is that if you settle a claim with the auto insurance company responsible, you will need to reimburse your health insurance company back for the medical bills they paid on your behalf that were a result of the accident.

This may sound like bad news, but there is some good news here as well. When you calculate the value of your claim, you use the total Invoice Amount (not the reduced amount the medical insurance companies pay). However, when you calculate the amount to pay back to the medical insurance company, you only need to pay them back the reduced amount.

We will now use our "Serious Injury" and "Minor Injury" examples to show how to determine how much money would need to be paid back to the medical insurance company involved. Table 4 shows the summary of medical bills from the serious injury example.

Table 4: "Serious Injuries" Medical Bills Claim Example (same as table 1).

	Invoice Amount	Insurance Paid Amount	Deductible Amount	Description	Service Date	Hospital / Dr. Name
	$1,500.00	$900.00	$100.00	Ambulance	Jan. 2	Ambulance Co.
	$100.00	$60.00	$10.00	X-ray	Jan. 2	Hosp. XYZ
	$2,500.00	$1,500.00	$250.00	Emerg. Rm	Jan. 2	Hosp. XYZ
	$8,000.00	$4,500.00	$400.00	Surgery	Jan. 3	Dr. QRS
	$5,500.00	$3,000.00	$255.00	Hospital	Jan. 3	Hosp. XYZ
	$1,250.00	$030.00	$100.00	Anesthesiologist	Jan. 3	Dr. BZD
	$100.00	$60.00	$10.00	X-ray	Jan. 3	Hosp. XYZ
	$475.00	$200.00	$100.00	Med. Supplies	Jan. 3	Hosp. XYZ
	$1,200.00	$600.00	$60.00	Therapy	Jan. 5	Clinic QRS
Total	$20,625.00	$11,470.00	$1,285.00			

In this example, the medical insurance company would demand to be reimbursed $11,470, which is the total amount in the "Insurance Paid Amount" column from the spreadsheet in Table 4. This is the pre-negotiated payment amount that they actually paid out for medical services and treatment. Once the injured person settles his/her claim, they would need to pay the medical insurance company $11,470 out of the claim money they received from the auto insurance company.

Table 5: "Minor Injuries" Medical Bills Claim Example (same as table 3).

	Invoice Amount	Insurance Paid Amount	Deductible Amount	Description	Service Date	Hospital / Dr. Name
	$1,500.00	$900.00	$100.00	Ambulance	Jan. 2	Ambulance Co.
	$100.00	$60.00	$10.00	X-ray	Jan. 2	Hosp. XYZ
	$2,500.00	$1,500.00	$250.00	Emerg. Rm	Jan. 2	Hosp. XYZ

	Invoice Amount	Insurance Paid Amount	Deductible Amount	Description	Service Date	Hospital / Dr. Name
	$475.00	$200.00	$60.00	Med. Supplies	Jan. 3	Hosp. XYZ
	$1,200.00	$600.00	$60.00	Therapy	Jan. 5	Clinic QRS
Total	$5,775.00	$3,260.00	$480.00			

In this example, the medical insurance company will demand to be reimbursed $3,260, which is the total amount in "Insurance Paid Amount" column from the spreadsheet in Table 5. Once the injured person settles the claim, they would need to pay the medical insurance company $3,260 out of the claim money they received from the auto insurance company.

Once you know the dollar amount of the medical lien, you need to check this figure. The lien amount should never be larger than the Total (bottom row) Insurance Paid Amount (third column from left) in the spreadsheet. If the lien amount is larger than this value in the spreadsheet, the insurer may have mistakenly included other medical bills in the lien amount. You will need to work with them to point out that those other medical bills were not related to the accident and have them removed from the lien.

Calculating the Value of Your Claim

Now it's time to figure out what your claim is worth. As I stated in the beginning of this chapter, the equation for calculating claim value is:

CLAIM VALUE = ((PAIN & SUFFERING + LOST INCOME + LOST OPPORTUNITY) X (% OF FAULT ATTRIBUTED TO OTHER PERSON)) – MEDICAL LIENS

Now that we have figured out how to calculate each item in the equation, let's fill in the values for our "Serious Injury" and "Minor Injury" examples. This will determine the total value of these two claims. In both scenarios, we will assume there is no lost opportunity and that the other party is 100% at fault.

SERIOUS INJURY CLAIM VALUE = (($82,500 + $2,000 + $0) X 100%) - $11,470 = $73,030

MINOR INJURY CLAIM VALUE = (($17,325 + $2,000 + $0) X 100%) - $3,260 = $16,065

Other Factors – What Would a Jury Award?

Other factors that might increase or decrease the value of your claim are the subjective points that would be presented in a court-of-law, which could influence what a jury would award. Just like there is no formula for how a jury would react to such items, there also is no formula for how these factors influence the award.

These other factors that could increase the value of your claim include:

- Were you a victim of a crime or gross negligence?
- Did the accident result in disfigurement or noticeable scarring?
- Did you suffer significant stress, for example, regarding how to provide for your family?
- Was your spousal relationship affected, commonly called loss of consortium?
- Would a jury react positively to you based on having a good driving record, or an honorable profession such as a schoolteacher; or would they feel sympathy toward you (for example a child or an elderly person)?

There are also other factors that can work against you. Examples would be if you had a bad driving record, a history of driving while intoxicated, a criminal record or long-term unemployment. All of these are examples that will reduce the value of the settlement.

If the "other factors" are in your favor, you may be able to increase the value of the multiplier to the high-end of the scale. For example, if you require two-years to recover, but do not have permanent damage, the low-end of the multiplier range is three, and other factors that are in your favor could increase the multiplier from a value of three to five.

Conversely, if these other factors are negative, the value of your claim is diminished. Negative factors that will cause you to be viewed unfavorably can easily reduce a claim that should have a multiplier of five to a multiplier of only two.

If you are determined to achieve a settlement at the high-end of the range, you need to work closely with an attorney. Without a serious threat of going to court, insurance companies will not pay the high-end value of pain and suffering.

Punitive Damages

Another factor that could increase your total claim value is punitive damages, which are specifically allowed under law for the case where the party at fault should be punished for what they have done. This is often the case if the other party caused intentional harm. Punitive damages may have the effect of doubling or tripling (called "treble" in lawyer lingo) the damages amount.

If you believe the person at fault acted willfully to hurt you, make sure you understand the laws in your state for punitive damages. In many cases, in order to qualify for punitive damages you need to specifically request punitive damages in your claim. Punitive damages may not be granted if you do not request this as part of the claim value.

Checklist of key points learned in this step:

- Review the accident report to determine if you have been assigned a portion, or a percentage, of the fault.
- Using the equation in this chapter, calculate the value of your claim.
- Track and total the amount your medical insurer paid for the medical bills in order to calculate the maximum amount of the medical liens they will expect to be reimbursed for.
- If you believe someone intentionally injured you, check the punitive damages laws for your state.

To Do:

1. _____

2. _____

3. _____

4. _____

Could I Lose Money on a PI Claim?

The simple answer is "no." You will not lose money on a PI claim if the claim is properly managed. Properly managing the claim comes down to not paying money for any services to help you with your claim. The main service that you may hire would be an attorney. If you hire an attorney, only compensate them based on a contingency fee (sometimes called "no win, no fee") agreement. This way you incur no costs, unless you win. The appropriate percentage to pay in this type of agreement is discussed in Chapter 8.

Legal Review

Having read the book up to this point, you have a good understanding of your claim's value. Meeting a PI attorney at this point will provide an independent opinion on the value of the claim as well as an understanding of how solid the claim may be and whether there may be any unique situations you need to consider. While meeting attorneys early in the process is recommended, you should not hire one until you have read Chapter 8 – Attorneys – Hiring, Compensating and Managing.

With regards to how solid the claim is, you can expect the attorney to explain how complicated the claim process will be (this is his sales pitch intended to establish value for his services). If the attorney pushes you to sign a contract, usually called a contingency fee agreement, saying he is your lawyer in this case, then this is an indication he believes the claim can be won. PI attorneys work on contingency fees, meaning they only get paid if you win. This means they are only interested in claims that are a sure bet for payment.

Whether you plan to hire an attorney or not, contacting an attorney early on is useful in case you need one in the future. As an example, the insurance company could drag out the negotiations and deny the claim or give a low-ball offer just as the statute of limitations is about to expire. Insurance companies intentionally do this because they know a lawsuit cannot be filed beyond the timeframe defined by the statute of limitations; meaning your claim becomes worthless. If the insurance company attempts to do this to you, you need to be in a position to hire an attorney on short notice. You will only be in a position to hire an attorney on short notice if you have already established a relationship with one.

Once you speak with an attorney by telephone, they will typically want to come meet you to get to know you better, learn more about the case and do a quick review of the police report, insurance policy and any other documentation you have. In this first meeting, you should provide all the information they request and discuss the attorney's opinion on the claims value, a realistic amount you can expect to recover considering local laws and the insurance policies in place, how he would ensure the amount you recover is in excess of any medical bills which must be paid, what he charges for compensation and what the process of recovering that money entails (insurance claim, lawsuit, etc.).

I recommend you meet with a minimum of two attorneys to ensure the information you are getting is correct. If they predict very different valuations on the claim and different outcomes, you need to understand why and assess if one does not understand or is trying to pull a fast one on you to get you to sign a contingency fee agreement.

Ask the attorney if there are special considerations under the law that would increase the amount you could recover. For example, if there was intentional wrongdoing, does your state have statutes entitling you to double (two times) or treble (three times) damages?

Don't let a lawyer push you into signing a contract that says he is the lawyer representing you in your claim. Wait until you are 100% sure that you don't want to represent yourself, and that this is the right person to represent you.

Checklist of key points learned in this step:

- Meet with attorneys early to help determine if the claim is worth pursuing.
- Ask the attorney the value of the claim and the process for resolving the claim.
- Ask about the statute of limitations and whether there are any unique considerations that could limit the time to file the claim (such as a government agency or municipality being involved).
- Ask if there are any special considerations that could change the value of the claim such as punitive damages or caps on insurance policies.

To Do:

1. _____

2. _____

3. _____

4. _____

Is the Claim Worth Filing?

It is now time to decide whether to pursue your claim. This section shows how to make this decision based solely on assessing how much money you could recover.

All financial discussions and example calculations from this point forward assume your objective is to settle a claim with an auto insurance company. Excluded from this analysis is the situation where your plan is to file a lawsuit against the party at fault. Filing a lawsuit is a different situation and beyond the scope of this book.

In order to determine how much insurance money you can recover, you need to know the policy limits of the insurance policies involved. These policy limits are for both the person at fault as well as your own UnderInsured Motorist coverage.

The reason you need to know the policy limits is for the situation when the person who is liable for your accident has a smaller insurance policy, or lower dollar limits, than your own insurance policy. Because they are at fault, their insurance pays first. However, if the other party's insurance policy is not enough to cover the amount of your claim, you can then turn to your own insurance policy to cover the remaining amount.

To help explain how this works, let's again use the Minor Injuries and Serious Injuries examples.

Example A

This is the Minor Injuries claim with a claim value of $19,325. The other party has a $50,000 policy limit and is 100% at fault.

With a policy limit of $50,000, the person filing the claim can expect to recover the full $19,325, but will need to pay medical liens of $3,260. This leaves them with $16,065 in their pocket.

CLAIM VALUE = ((PAIN & SUFFERING + LOST INCOME + LOST OPPORTUNITY) X (% OF FAULT ATTRIBUTED TO OTHER PERSON)) – MEDICAL LIENS

CLAIM VALUE = $19,325 - $3,260 = $16,065

If they hired an attorney, they would share the attorney costs (assumed at 33%) with the medical insurer. This means they would reduce both the medical lien amount and what they keep by 33%. To do this, they would multiply each amount by 1 – 33% = 67%. The medical reimbursement amount becomes $3,260 x 67% = $2,184. The amount the person filing the claim keeps becomes $16,065 x 67% = $10,764.

CLAIM VALUE WITH AN ATTORNEY INVOLVED = $16,065 X 67%
= $10,764.

Now let's take a look at how this works in a scenario where the claim value is more than the other party's insurance policy limit and you have UnderInsured Motorist (UIM) coverage as part of your own insurance policy.

Example B

The person filing the claim has serious injuries. The other party has a $50,000 policy limit and the person hurt has UIM coverage of $100,000.

In the Serious Injuries example, the claim value was $84,500 before deducting medical liens. With a policy limit of $50,000, they can expect to recover the full $50,000 from the other party's insurance company. After recovering the full amount, they would then file an additional UIM claim against their own insurance company. They could recover an additional $34,500 from their own insurance company, totaling the full $84,500. From this settlement, they would pay the medical liens of $11,470, leaving $73,030 in their pocket.

CLAIM VALUE = $84,500 - $11,470 = $73,030.

If they hired an attorney, they and the medical insurer would share in the attorney's fees (again assumed at 33%).

To calculate this amount, multiply by 1 – 33% = 67%. The medical reimbursement amount becomes $11,470 x 67% = $7,685. The amount the person filing the claim keeps becomes $73,030 x 67% = $48,930.

Based on the examples above and the insurance policies involved, you can now calculate the amount of money you expect to recover. Read on if the dollar amount is worth the effort of filing a claim.

Taxes

When you consider the dollar amounts listed above, it is important to understand that money paid by an insurance policy for damages is generally not taxable. There are exceptions to this such as repairing or replacing property that is deducted as a business expense, or personal injury or bad faith cases where punitive damages are applied, so you need to get financial and tax advice from a professional.

Tax advice is beyond the scope of this book because it often depends on your personal situation, is complicated and frequently changes. For these reasons, you need to check with a tax specialist to ensure any money received from insurance settlements is properly handled when you report income.

Checklist of key points learned in this section:

- Compare the claim value to the applicable insurance policies to determine what you can reasonably recover.
- Deduct the medical bills you will need to refund to the medical insurance provider.
- Check with your tax specialist to determine if the money would be taxable to you.
- If the money you can expect to recover is worth the effort, read on.
- If the money you can expect to recover is not worth the effort, read Chapters 10 and 11 to understand the dysfunction of the insurance industry, what consumers can do about the situation and how you can protect yourself.

To Do:

1. _____

2. _____

3. _____

4. _____

5. _____

The Inside Story - #1

The stories related in these "Inside Story" sections are factual accounts of events that took place during the claim process following my accident. These stories are included in order to help you understand how insurance companies behave, enabling you to be better prepared to win your claim.

Delays, Denials, Dishonesty and Deceit

One of the first interactions I had with my auto insurance company came when I filed a claim for Medical Payments Coverage (MPC), which is medical insurance for you or passengers in your vehicle, independent of who is at fault. Many auto insurance policies have MPC included, often with coverage ranging between $1,000 and $25,000, per person. In my case, I had $25,000 of MPC coverage and as soon as my medical bills topped $25,000, I was eligible to receive this payment.

The Claims Representative: Friendly and Professional

I topped the threshold of $25,000 on the second day in the hospital's intensive care unit. When back at home, I collected the invoices from the hospital stay and sent a registered letter, including copies of the medical bills, to the claims representative. Upon receiving my letter, the claims representative called me and was very nice, helpful, caring and knowledgeable. In short, I trusted her. I was pleased that she was working for my insurance company and would be "helping me."

That Claims Representative Only Pretended to Help

What I came to find out as time passed was this nice, helpful, caring and knowledgeable person was anything but nice, helpful and caring. I had provided all my medical bills, with all the detailed information about procedures, billing codes, doctors, etc. I provided everything the hospital was able to provide to me. Even with all this information in hand, the claims representative insisted there was more information they needed to approve the claim payment.

To resolve the issue, I got the exact information she said the insurance company needed and called the hospital to request this information. The hospital personnel explained to me this information was not available and they could not get it. The insurance company would not accept this explanation so I set up a conference call between the claims representative, the hospital personnel and myself. On the call, a hospital employee explained that the request was not in line with standard industry operating procedures and unreasonable since it was not possible for any hospital to provide the information requested.

After the hospital employee dropped off the line, the insurance company representative reiterated that they could not make the payment without receiving this information. With clear statements from hospital personnel that the information requested was not how the industry operates, and not possible to provide, the insurance company obviously knew they were making it impossible for me to collect on my insurance policy. In other words, they were intentionally delaying and denying legitimate claims. The objective of delays and denials such as the ones in this example is to wear the person making the claim down. In this first claim it worked. They had worn me down. I stopped pursuing the claim.

Checklist of key points learned in this Inside Story:

- Delaying and denying is a common tactic used by insurance companies. Think of it as a way of intentionally torturing you, to wear you down so you settle for less money to end the pain of dealing with them.
- Keep detailed notes of every conversation you have with an insurance company (Appendix C has an example form for doing this). Include whom you spoke with, when the conversation took place and the detail of what was discussed. Record the conversation if you can, but to do this, you need to get their permission. In the example above, I kept the name, date and topics discussed for each and every call. These records were important later in the process when they began changing explanations.

To Do:

1. _____

2. _____

3. _____

My Auto Insurer Modified My Medical Records!

Nine months after the accident, I was still far from a full recovery. I experienced constant neck and hip pain. I walked into a doctor's office hardly turning my head due to a neck that hurt continuously and limping due to severe hip pain. The doctor was a world-renowned hip specialist with expertise in the surgery I needed as a result of the accident.

I was standing as the doctor entered the examination room. However, I wasn't standing to be polite. I was standing because it hurt more to sit than to stand. During this visit, I recounted the events that had taken place and the injuries I had sustained. The doctor could tell without even examining me that I had real physical problems and needed help. Interestingly, one of his very first questions was "who is your auto insurance company?" I told him their name and he responded immediately with "you need an attorney." Along with this statement, he presented his credentials and why he believed I needed an attorney. His credentials were impressive in that he was not only a highly-regarded hip doctor, but he also did consulting work for insurance companies, including mine, as an Independent Medical Expert. He knew the inner workings of the insurance industry.

This recommendation to get an attorney didn't resonate with me at the time because I was not interested in money. I was interested in recovering. Thus, while the doctor provided me with the name of a PI attorney, I didn't bother to call. I planned to recover, then settle a reasonable claim (it still didn't matter to me how much the financial recovery was). I just wanted to fully recover.

The Surgery.... and the Doctor's Notes

While no serious medical procedure is anything other than memorable, this hip surgery was particularly memorable for a number of reasons. It was the medical records following this surgery that the insurance company modified to make it look like I had been lying and was not really injured in the accident. Yes, they actually modified my medical records. The following is what they did:

Immediately following the 3.5 hour-long surgery, I awakened with searing pain in both eyes. The pain was a sharp, piercing pain so overpowering I could not open my eyes at all. Somehow I had gotten corneal abrasions in both eyes during the operation and had to be seen by an eye doctor each day for the next four days. I had been a long-term patient of the eye doctor so he had notes from all of my annual checkups. During my routine visit two years before, I told him that I had ridden a 129-mile bike ride called "The Death Ride." Little did I know at the time, but he put this information in his notes even though it had nothing to do with my eyes. This is the information the lawyers manipulated!

My Insurance Company's Attorney Modified My Medical Records

While the dates were clearly marked in my eye doctor's notes, the insurance company's attorney modified the dates and stated that I rode the 129-mile ride in the months following my accident, not two years prior as the doctor's notes clearly stated. The insurance company's attorney was trying to establish that I was not badly hurt and damage my credibility. The reality was that I was flat on my back in bed recovering from the accident when the Death Ride took place the year of my accident.

In writing this book, I consulted with several attorneys, as well as other consumer advocates, working for the benefit of policyholders. When I relate this story, not a single one of them was surprised. Their response is usually something like "don't feel picked on or persecuted, this is normal behavior for insurance companies." Attorneys I consulted with while writing this book even stated that the insurance company attorney who took these actions should be disbarred (his license to work as an attorney revoked) and the insurance company should pay serious fines.

For me, this was the turning point from simply wanting to settle a claim, versus being on a mission to hold the insurance company accountable for their actions.

Checklist of key points learned in this section:

- Proactively ask your doctors how your insurance companies (auto and medical) behave in personal injury cases. If they are reputed to behave badly, shop around for a better insurance company.
- Check the Consumer Reviews section of the Injured Money website at, www.injuredmoney.com. As data is collected on insurance companies, we will publish the results of the reviews people provide.
- Thoroughly review all medical records provided to insurance companies. Remove any and all information that is from a different time period, or is not relevant to the claim.

To Do:

1. _____

2. _____

3. _____

My Medical Insurer Refused to Pay Medical Bills

Before having hip surgery, I got all the appropriate approvals from my medical insurance carrier. Having their approval, I proceeded forward with an expensive operation. Following the operation, a medical insurance company employee called me and asked if some of my medical bills were related to an automobile accident. While it concerned me that they were asking this question, I was not going to be dishonest with them so I told them, yes. I questioned him on why this mattered and if there could be any impact on my coverage. He stated that this was just a routine question they ask, then thanked me for the information and I heard nothing more.

Several months later, my doctor complained to me that the medical insurance company had not yet paid him. I responded that it must be a mistake since everything had been pre-approved and that I would look into why there was a delay. Much to my dismay, I learned my health insurance company stopped paying my medical bills without informing me they were going to do this. I soon learned I was now personally responsible for over $84,000 of medical bills.

Shortly thereafter, I started receiving letters demanding immediate payment from the various medical providers, including the supplier of medical implants used in the surgery, the anesthesiologist, and others, all stating they would report me to collections agencies. I felt betrayed. My employer paid for medical insurance and I contributed every pay period for this insurance coverage. Furthermore, my medical insurance company had pre-approved these expenses, but now smugly told me their pre-approval was not really an obligation to pay.

I checked the benefit book to understand the policy for this situation. What I learned was that according to our contract, the medical insurance company should have asked me to sign a statement saying they had a lien on my medical payments. This form would have stated that if I collected money from another insurance company, or responsible party, I would have to pay them back. I requested the medical insurance provider to send me this document but they refused. I now needed to immediately come up with $84,000.

I called the sales representative that sold the policy to our company. She was very positive and professed her desire and willingness to help get the situation resolved. She introduced me to another person responsible for this type of situation who told me they would not pay the medical bills and they would not discuss it further. I went through their official appeals process, but got the same response.

This was a flagrant disregard for the contract we had. Within the contract, they stated: In the case someone else is responsible, they would ask me to sign a third-party-liability form obligating me to pay them back when, and if, I recovered the money. But they refused to honor this contract.

To understand this issue better and what you can do if this happens to you, read "Chapter 5 – What to Do if Your Medical Insurer Stops Paying Bills."

In this Inside Story section, you have learned the following:

- Medical Insurance companies may refuse to honor their contract (the policy) with you.
- Insurance agents are unable to influence their company when it comes to settling a claim or honoring contracts.

Chapter 5 – What to Do if Your Insurer Stops Paying Medical Bills

Having a medical insurer stop paying your medical bills can be devastating. Hopefully, you won't need to deal with this unfortunate situation. Statistics show that the number one cause of people filing bankruptcy is medical bills. If this does not concern you, go to Chapter 6.

If your health insurer stopped paying your bills, then you are almost certainly early in the process and have not yet filed an auto insurance claim. In this situation, the need to pay medical bills becomes urgent. Hence, we will cover the topic of what to do when the medical insurer stops paying medical bills first, then cover how to win your auto insurance claim(s) in Chapter 6.

Settling Medical Liens and Medical Bills – Three Scenarios

First, what is a medical lien? A lien is a legal right to money received in the future from the party liable. Now in English: When the other driver hit you, their insurance company became liable, or responsible, for all costs associated with the accident. This means they need to pay medical bills. Since your medical insurance company is already set up to pay medical bills, they typically keep paying these bills. When you receive a settlement from the other driver's auto insurance company, you owe the cost of the medical bills back to the medical insurance company. This legal obligation to pay that money is a medical lien.

One of three scenarios will be faced when settling medical liens and medical bills.

The first scenario is that the medical insurer paid the expenses and is looking to recover whatever they can, assuming you file a claim with an auto insurance company. The medical insurance policy will specify if you are required to reimburse the medical insurer. The amount is negotiable and the medical insurer will likely settle for less than their actual cost since anything they recover is upside for them, and if you are working directly with them, they are not incurring legal expenses. To resolve this situation, negotiate directly with the insurance company.

The second scenario is that the medical insurance company contacted you after the accident and inquired whether the bills were related to an auto accident. Upon hearing it was related to an auto accident, they requested you to sign an agreement stating you will reimburse them if and when you settle a claim with the auto insurance company. This is known as receiving treatment on a lien basis. To verify how much money you owe them, we will look at Table 6 below.

Table 6: Verifying the Total Amount Due to Reimburse Medical Liens.

	Invoice Amount	Insurance Paid Amount	Deductible Amount	Description	Service Date	Hospital / Dr. Name
	$1,500.00	$900.00	$100.00	Ambulance	Jan. 2	Ambulance Co.
	$100.00	$60.00	$10.00	X-ray	Jan. 2	Hosp. XYZ
	$2,500.00	$1,500.00	$250.00	Emerg. Rm	Jan. 2	Hosp. XYZ
	$475.00	$200.00	$60.00	Med. Supplies	Jan. 3	Hosp. XYZ
	$1,200.00	$600.00	$60.00	Therapy	Jan. 5	Clinic QRS
Total	$5,775.00	$3,260.00	$480.00			

In this table, the column titled Insurance Paid Amount contains what the insurance company paid for the treatment you received. As noted in Chapter 4, the medical insurance company doesn't pay the full amount billed by your hospital or doctor, but pays a pre-negotiated, reduced rate. Your reimbursement to the medical insurer is based on this reduced rate, which in the example shown in table 6 totals $3,260. The statements mailed to you by the insurance company will include this reduced rate so all that is required is to add up these amounts.

The medical insurance company will also provide the total amount. However, expenses unrelated to the accident frequently get inadvertently included so it is recommended you check their figures. If you can show the insurance company's amounts are inflated, or high, that will result in you keeping more of the money.

The third scenario is that the medical insurance company refuses to pay the medical providers and the auto insurance company is not accepting the bills so the liability is yours.

The first two scenarios are straightforward so this chapter will not discuss them in further detail. The focus for the remainder of the chapter will be on how to resolve the third scenario, which is the trickiest. We will use my case as the example of how to work through this situation.

It All Started with a Credit Collections Notice in the Mail

Several months after the accident, I began a new job which came with a new medical insurance provider. I was still undergoing a number of different treatments and racking up significant medical bills.

Even though the medical insurance company had pre-approved the treatments and dollar amounts, they stopped paying the bills and didn't bother to notify me. When I first received notification from the doctors, and others who were owed money, that they were holding me responsible, the payments were already late. In multiple cases, the first notification arrived in the form of a threat to turn over the bills to a collections agency. While this was concerning, the moment of truth came when I realized the total amount due was $84,000. Eighty-four thousand dollars the medical insurer refused to pay.

Because I was still far from being fully recovered, I hadn't begun to consider filing an auto insurance claim. Until the long-term effects of the injuries were understood, it was premature to think about settling with an auto insurance company.

Between a Rock and a Hard Spot

I was truly stuck between the proverbial rock and a hard spot. The bills were large and were due immediately. I had no prospects of receiving a claim settlement anytime in the foreseeable future.

I didn't have a clue what to do. I had many questions about the predicament I found myself in. How much money could I get from an auto insurance settlement? How much money did I actually need to pay?

The first step was to break the problem down into smaller pieces, including: medical providers to whom I owed money, insurance companies where I may be able to get money and whether I should take on this challenge myself or hire an attorney.

Medical Providers

Communicating with medical providers was critical. Their cooperation was essential in order to reach an agreeable solution. I knew my communication with them needed to be both sincere and convincing and that I needed to communicate with them immediately.

I contacted each medical provider by telephone. Telephone calls are much more effective in a situation like this because the person you are speaking with can connect in a way that is difficult to do via electronic communication.

I explained the situation and let them know I had received a notification that I owed them money. I told them that my medical insurance company had pre-approved the payments and then without notifying me, refused to pay. I let them know that in total, I suddenly owed nearly a $100,000 in medical bills (I recommend rounding the figures up and not giving exact amounts).

I re-assured the representatives from the medical providers that I was taking their needs seriously, and needed them to work with me. I shared with them my plans to file a claim with the auto insurance company of the woman who hit me, while being honest with them that I did not know when it would settle, or for how much. I asked for them to give me time to work through the claim. Because I didn't know how long this would take, my promise to them was to communicate with them regularly so they knew the status of the claim. All of the medical providers agreed.

The medical providers' cooperation was encouraging. All eight medical providers, spanning from doctors with their own individual practice to large corporations, were understanding of my predicament and committed to work with me. I knew I had an opportunity to successfully resolve this bad situation. Now it was up to me to deliver on my promises.

Attorneys

The problem of how to pay eight medical providers without yet having a settlement from an auto insurance company seemed like an interesting challenge so I decided to take it upon myself rather than hiring an attorney. Besides, I knew that if I didn't succeed at solving the problem, I still had the option of bringing in an attorney to finalize what I started.

If you have a PI attorney interested in taking on your case, you will want to consider the cost. We looked at how to do the calculations of the cost of having an attorney involved in Chapter 4, so I only include a simple description here addressing the uniqueness of this situation: The PI attorney's fees will be a percentage (nominally 33%) of the settlement amount from the insurance policy. The medical providers and lien holders will share in this cost, meaning they will reduce their charge by 33%. This way you do not bear the full cost of the attorney.

The key consideration for you is what the attorney's fees will be based on. At a minimum, the attorney will expect a fee for the full value of the first auto insurance company settlement. If an additional UIM settlement is a consideration, your agreement with the attorney will need to be specific about whether the fee applies to that settlement as well.

Insurance Companies

The first step is to go back to the medical insurer with the goal of getting them to pay the bills. Be sure to pursue this option fully by taking the following steps:

- Speak with your contact at the insurance company.
- Speak to their manager.
- File an appeal with the insurance company.
- Share your experience about the company on the Injured Money website in the Consumer Reviews so other people know what to expect from them.
- If they still do not respond positively, report them to the state insurance commissioner.

If the medical insurer agrees to pay the bills, you now have the flexibility to wait before filing a claim with the auto insurer. But if the medical insurer does not agree to pay the bills, do not wait hoping for a positive response. Take the next step and move on to pursue a claim with the auto insurer at fault in the accident. To do this, follow the guidance in Chapter 6 on how to prepare and file the claim, negotiate and settle an agreement.

Negotiating with Multiple Parties, Simultaneously

Negotiating with several parties simultaneously can be intimidating, but in reality, it's not that difficult. The first step is to know how much money you have to work with. This means you need to settle the claim with the auto insurance company before you can finalize negotiations with the medical providers.

When dealing with the auto insurance company, take special care not to let them know you are under pressure to settle this agreement. If the auto insurance company knows you are under pressure, their delays will become even more extreme. The auto insurer knows that the longer they delay, the more the pressure on you mounts, making you more likely to accept a small, undervalued offer.

Once the claim with the auto insurer is settled, you have the money to pay the medical providers. If the auto insurance settlement was more than the amount due to the medical providers, then it is simply a matter of determining a fair amount. One way to determine a fair amount is to use the amount the medical insurance company would have paid.

In my case, this first auto insurance settlement was only $50,000, which was capped by the policy limit. In this scenario, the medical providers needed to take an average of a 40% reduction in order for all bills to be paid. However, I knew one of the medical providers would not take any discount. This particular provider told me up front that their services were in high demand and that they did not discount for insurance companies. That meant in order to pay all medical providers, all the others needed to agree to a 50% discount from the invoice amount.

A 50% discount from the invoice amount seemed as if it may be possible since it was only slightly below the 30% to 45% discount insurance companies often negotiate. Based on this information, I prepared the following request for the medical providers:

- Accept an average of 50% reduction from the invoice amount.

- If agreed, then I would accept the auto insurer's settlement offer and they would get paid immediately.

- They needed to agree this deal was final and forgo any rights to further compensation. This meant it would not be necessary to file a UIM claim to pay them more.

I reached out to the same contact person I had spoken with before at each of the creditors and informed them that I had come to an agreement with the auto insurance company. I explained the agreement (the three points outlined above) and explained the benefits were that the payment amount was similar to what the medical insurance company would have paid and they would get paid quickly if everyone agreed. If a party did not agree, then an attorney would be required, resulting in everyone receiving less money as well as a longer delay before receiving any money.

I was pleasantly surprised that all the medical providers were cooperative. It took a few weeks to finalize all of the agreements since everyone needed to participate and the discounts involved required approval within their organizations. In the end, all medical providers involved accepted what I believe was a reasonable discount. I got agreements in writing from each medical provider with new invoices for the adjusted amounts along with a statement that this was the final and total amount. With this, I paid them.

Checklist of key points learned in this chapter:

- Don't be intimidated by this problem. Settling with the medical providers is much easier than settling with an auto insurance company. Make your step-by-step plan of how to address the issues in your situation and get started.
- Identify the conclusion to the multiple party negotiations that you believe would be acceptable to everyone, and then confirm with the other parties they would settle for this amount.
- Maintain regular communication with the parties whom you are negotiating.
- Meet the commitments you make so they know they can trust you.

To Do:

1. _____

2. _____

3. _____

4. _____

Chapter 6 – How to Win Your Claim(s)

Congratulations on your decision to move forward. This chapter will guide you step-by-step through the process of filing, negotiating and settling your claim. These steps include:

Step 1 - Immediate Actions to Move Forward

Step 2 - Preparing and Filing the Claim with the Other Party

Step 3 - Negotiating Your Claim

Step 4 - Settling with the Other Party

Step 5 - Updating the Claim to a UIM Claim with Your Insurer

You may still be wondering if you need an attorney. Before making that decision, read through this chapter so you have a complete understanding of what's ahead. If you feel an attorney may be the right approach for you, then go to Chapter 8 where you will learn how to hire, compensate and manage an attorney.

Step 1 – Immediate Actions to Move Forward

As you tackle the claims process, the first step includes understanding the laws of your state, communicating your plan to the insurance company and making sure your files are complete and organized. In step 2 of this chapter, you will begin drawing on the complete and organized files discussed in Chapter 2, the section titled "Preparation: Enabling You to Win Your Claim."

On the legal side, there are two key laws you must be aware of before moving forward. The first is whether you reside in a "no-fault" state and the second is the statute of limitations for your state (if the accident were in another state, the laws of that state may apply). The following sections discuss these laws.

No-Fault

No-fault insurance is not offered in most states. At the time of this publication there are 12 no-fault states in the U.S. If you live in one of these no-fault states, it is recommended you read the Personal Injury Protection (PIP) section of your insurance policy. This section of the policy will define the process for filing your claim. If the policy is not clear, you should check with your insurance company or agent.

Whether you live in a state that has no-fault insurance or not, the steps outlined in this book on how to value, file and negotiate a claim, hire and work with an attorney, etc., all apply. The difference for a no-fault state is that you will likely file a claim with your own insurance company first. The differences in filing a claim with your own insurance company vs. the other party's insurance company are described in Step 5 of this chapter. Read this step before filing your claim. In my case, I did not file with my own insurance company first because I did not live in a no-fault state. I filed first with the insurance company of the person who was at fault. This is the most common scenario.

Statute of Limitations

Every state has a statute of limitations that defines the maximum amount of time allowed to file a lawsuit after the accident has occurred. While the focus of this chapter is on filing a claim, it is critical to know the statue of limitations in order to ensure you have the option of filing a lawsuit. Reasons you may need to file a lawsuit include:

- The insurance company is unresponsive and refuses to negotiate a settlement.

- The insurance company offers you a settlement that is too low.

In the situations described above, you may need to file a lawsuit in order to force a settlement or to force a reasonable settlement. If you fail to file a lawsuit before the deadline defined by the statute of limitations, you lose the right to file a lawsuit. And, without the threat of a lawsuit, your claim becomes worthless because the insurance company knows you have no recourse.

Typically, the statute of limitations is two to three years, but it can be as much as six years and as little as one year. To check the statute of limitations in your state (at the time of publication of this book) refer to Appendix F. For more up-to-date information visit the Laws by State page on the Injured Money website at www.injuredmoney.com, where laws and available resources are identified by state.

If you are filing a claim against a government agency, such as a city, county or state, for having known hazardous conditions that contributed to your injuries, your deadline for filing a lawsuit is likely much shorter than with an insurance company. Filing claims and lawsuits against a public entity will often need to be done within six months or less. To get the exact time requirements, check directly with the organization or a local attorney.

Given the statute of limitations, it is important that you begin your claims process as soon as you have a complete understanding of your injuries. If you wait to start the process as the deadline defined by the statute of limitations approaches, you will not have enough time to prepare, file and negotiate a fair and reasonable settlement. This gives the insurance company an advantage and they will likely respond with a low-ball offer or a flat denial. By starting the process well in advance of the statute of limitations expiring, you have time to file a claim, negotiate a settlement and if required, file a lawsuit.

Communicating Your Plan

Once the decision to file a claim is made, let the insurance company that you will be filing the claim against know your intentions. You should make your communication with them friendly, but firm. You want them to know that you are knowledgeable, confident and are not going to settle for anything less than a fair offer. You can let the insurance company know your plans by either a letter or a telephone call to your claims representative. However, you should not give them any information beyond the fact that you plan to file a claim.

It may seem that telling the insurance company of your intentions gives them time to prepare, but no matter when you tell them, they will take their time to prepare. Time is on their side and their goal is to delay the process in an effort to frustrate you into accepting a smaller settlement or until the statute of limitations expires and you have no recourse. This chapter explains how to manage the process to eliminate the advantages the insurance companies have over you based on both the laws and their experience.

Organization.... The Key to Success

Make sure all of your supporting documents are available and organized. This may sound like a simple task, but you would be surprised how often a lack of organization can cause a good claim to lose value. The organization on your part demonstrates to the insurance company that you are knowledgeable and that you would be viewed as a credible person if your case went to court.

As part of being organized, make sure to document every conversation with insurance company representatives. Their unresponsiveness, misleading communication and outright dishonesty are often critical factors in winning a bad faith lawsuit against an insurance company. Appendix C has a form for documenting each conversation. The form can be used as a guide for the information you need to collect and to capture the information if you are writing by hand. You should use whatever method, such as a computer or a notepad beside the phone that is easiest for you. Making this process simple will result in more thorough notes.

Checklist of key points learned in this step:

- Check your policy, or with your insurance agent, to determine if you have no-fault insurance. If so, the claim process will be defined by your policy.
- Know the statute of limitations as it applies to your accident.
- Communicate your intent to file a claim in a friendly, but firm tone. Do not give any information about the demands you will make when you file the claim. The detailed information will be provided with the claim you file.
- If you are still recovering, continue to keep detailed notes about your condition.
- Keep detailed notes documenting every conversation with insurance company representatives.
- Make sure your filing system is well organized by keeping copies of both the documentation that is sent to you and documents you send to others.

To Do:

1. _____

2. _____

3. _____

4. _____

5. _____

Step 2 – Preparing and Filing Your Claim with the Other Party

The claim you submit to the insurance company will consist of a demand letter and the necessary supporting documentation. The demand letter is the cover letter in which you explain the accident and its consequences, and specify the expected compensation. This letter will be part of the permanent record in all proceedings from this point forward. For this reason, it is important that the demand letter be: accurate, complete and clearly state the compensation expected.

In addition to describing all the important details about the accident, the demand letter also functions as the organizing document for the claim. With a good demand letter, the reader knows:

- What happened
- Who was at fault
- What injuries you suffered
- The cost of treating your injuries
- Your lost income
- Your lost opportunities
- What you expect as compensation
- The deadline for replying

In addition to stating these important points, the demand letter needs to include attachments for the supporting documentation, such as medical bills and lost income that are necessary to prove every point asserted in the letter.

Even if you plan to hire an attorney, you should write the initial draft of the demand letter because no one knows what happened to you better than you. The demand letter is your opportunity to tell your story. This is one of the first documents that will be read by claims representatives, their managers, attorneys, mediators, arbitrators and judges. You will never again get their undivided attention to tell your story. Furthermore, you will never meet some of these people. Make it count!

The Demand Letter

Before you begin writing the demand letter, you should go back and review the notes you kept following the accident that describe what took place, what other people said, the pain you experienced, etc. Refreshing your memory on these items will help you write a more powerful demand letter. Next, get out the expanding file folder where you have been collecting the information about your claim. Begin drawing on this information and put it together in the way that best represents your claim.

Writing the demand letter and preparing the claim goes through all the same topics covered in the "Valuing Your Claim" section of Chapter 4. The difference is that in Chapter 4 we discussed how to calculate the value of the claim and in this chapter we will review the description of the accident and events that followed, and the documents necessary to support the numbers and calculations from Chapter 4.

The length of the demand letter is not a measure of impact. You want it to be as succinct as possible, while describing the full impact the accident had on you, and the injuries that resulted from the accident. The following is an outline of the sections that will make up your demand letter:

Establishing Fault

The opening paragraph of the demand letter needs to explain what happened and establish who was at fault. To win your claim, you must convincingly prove that the other party was at fault. In a situation where the police report assigns fault to both parties, you will either need to agree to that allocation of fault, or have a strong case for arguing more fault should be allocated to the other party. If it is determined you are 100% at fault, you do not have a claim.

In discussion of who's at fault, reference any documentation you have that establishes fault such as the police report, a diagram of the accident scene and signed witness statements. If you are attaching a police report, make certain you understand to which party the report attributes fault, or responsibility, for the accident. If no police report is available, you will need signed, unbiased witness statements along with a diagram of the accident pictorially describing what took place.

Your Injuries and Long-Term Prognosis

In this section of the letter, you need to provide a complete description of the injuries. If the injuries are permanent or disfiguring, be sure to point this out since it can have a significant impact on how your injuries are valued. The severity of the injuries can be emphasized with real examples of limitations you have and will suffer as a result of the accident. As proof of the injuries, you can quote directly from the doctor's reports. However, you should be aware that quoting from a report will likely lead to a request for the entire report, so make sure the report is in no way damaging to you before referencing it in the demand letter.

The attachments referenced in this section of the letter may be minimal when filing with the other party's insurer because you are not obligated to provide doctors' reports or to be examined by their doctors. However, if you don't provide doctors' reports, you may not be able to convince the insurance company that your injuries justify the compensation demanded.

If you do not submit doctors' reports with the demand letter, you will most likely need to provide more complete medical information during the upcoming claim negotiation process. Be prepared for this by having a complete set of doctor reports available and making sure there is no information included in the reports that could damage your claim. Damaging information could include information about a pre-existing condition or even comments you made to the doctor about how quickly you were recovering. Often times in an accident, the patient will report how great they feel but then take a turn for the worse as they realize the full extent of their injuries. On the day you felt great, the doctor may have included these statements in the medical report and later on the insurance company could use them against you to prove you were not hurt as badly as you claimed.

Ask your doctor to include any permanent, residual effects in the medical report he makes following each treatment or office visit. This is an important request since doctors do not automatically include this information in their notes.

Collect all your medical records; read and understand them thoroughly in advance of filing the claim. Doctors typically provide these reports to you at no charge. Hospitals often charge a small handling fee for copying and mailing the medical records. Getting the detailed reports can take anywhere from two to eight weeks. Make sure you allow for this time in your schedule.

Total Medical Costs

In this section, write a brief description of the treatments you received, concluding with the total cost of the medical treatment.

The attachments in this section will be the invoices from the medical providers who treated you. This is the information you collected using the spreadsheet in Appendix E with hard copies in the file folder.

Through the course of getting second opinions, you may have seen doctors who didn't ultimately treat you. If these doctors had differing opinions on the problems you were suffering and the course of treatment necessary, do not include invoices from them. You should only include bills from the doctors who treated you or whose report helps your claim. It's best not to present any information that an insurance company can use to raise questions.

Lost Income

In this section, describe how much time you missed at work and what this translates into for total lost wages. If you took vacation or sick time and still got paid by your employer, this is considered lost income.

The attachments for this section should be a letter from your human resources or payroll department, documenting the actual time missed at work and the income associated with this amount of time. Keep in mind that if you are filing with the other party's insurance company, you do not have any contractual obligation to provide these work records. Practically speaking though, you will need to provide evidence for them to validate your claim of lost income so it's okay to include this information when you are filing with the other party's insurance company as long as you have made sure there is nothing damaging to you in the information you share.

Lost Opportunities

You only need to include this section if you intend to claim that you suffered lost business opportunities as a result of your accident. If you do intend to claim this, you need to make sure you have documentation that proves the opportunity was real and that it would have generated a specific amount of income. In this section, you should describe the opportunity fully and reference any supporting documents you have such as a written agreement or a statement from a third party that confirms you indeed had this opportunity and it was "lost" due to the accident.

Other Damages

In this section, you should include any specific events you missed or relationships that were impacted that had a negative impact on your life. Items to include here could be a family vacation you missed, the negative impact on a personal or professional relationship, or a poor performance review on your job due to lost time at work.

Compensation / Value of Your Claim

This is the section where you include the dollar amount you expect to be compensated for your injury. This compensation amount should be twice (or double) the amount you calculated in Chapter 4 on "Valuing Your Claim." The reason you need to start with an amount larger than what you expect to receive is because you need to leave room for negotiation. The insurance company will negotiate with you throughout the process with the objective of paying you the least amount possible. Thus, by starting with a demand that is double what you really expect, you leave room to negotiate back-and-forth a few times in order to receive a fair settlement.

Deadline for a Reply

In this section, you need to specify a deadline by which the insurance company needs to respond to your demand letter. When filing with the other party's insurance company, give roughly 30 calendar days. Because you have no contract with the other party's insurance company, they have no right to collect information such as medical or work records. The only thing they need to do is read your file, ask questions and propose a settlement.

No matter what insurance company you are dealing with, if the statute of limitations is approaching, you need to be sure your deadline for a reply is a couple of months before the statute of limitations expires. This is the only way you can be assured of having time to prepare and file a lawsuit if they do not reply by your deadline or if they respond with a low-ball offer.

Property Damage is Not Included in this Demand Letter

While you can claim the loss of personal property damaged in the accident, this is a separate claim with a different claims representative and is therefore not included in this demand letter. For more information on filing a property damage claim, see Appendix B.

Be sure when you file a property damage claim that you do not sign a release of liability that includes your PI claim. While it is acceptable to release all liability on the automobile once the repairs have been made, do not release the insurance company of any liability for your pain and suffering.

Sample Demand Letter

Following is a sample demand letter that describes a fictitious claim. To maintain consistency in the examples used, the dollar amounts and injuries described match the example claim called "Serious Injury" that we covered in Chapter 4.

Letter 2: Sample Demand Letter

Today's Date

Your Name
Address

Claim representative's name
Title

Insurance company name
Address

Re: Name, "your insured" (this is the name of the insurance company's insured)

Claimant: Your name
Claim #:

Date of loss:

Dear: "claim representative's name"

I was injured in an automobile accident with your insured (other driver's name) on (give the date and time) in (name the town). I was heading (direction) on (street name), traveling at a safe speed of 25 mph (the speed limit on this section of road is 25 mph). As I traveled through the intersection of (street name) with a green light granting my the right-of-way, your insured approached from the other direction. Suddenly, without warning (such as a turn indicator) your insured ignored the red light from his direction and abruptly turned left – immediately in front of me – crossing my path as he turned. I hit the brakes as quickly and as hard as I could, but skidded directly into the passenger side of his car. My car came to an abrupt stop when our cars collided. The impact of the collision caused my body to hurtle forward, breaking my right arm above the wrist.

The report filed by the police officer that came to the scene of the accident cited multiple witnesses saying your insured ran a red light to make the left-hand turn. These witnesses also stated that I was traveling at a safe speed, on the proper side of the road. Your insured was cited for reckless driving. The police report, establishing your insured as 100% at-fault, is included as Attachment A.

I was taken to the hospital where I had surgery for a compound fracture, held overnight, and then released to go home. The doctor prescribed pain medication for my arm. I was on pain medication for one week and unable to drive a car during this time due to the medication. I had eight weeks of therapy, two times per week. My medical expenses are included as Attachment B. The total medical expense is $20,625.

I missed five days of work due to the accident. My hourly rate is $50 per hour for total lost wages of $2,000. Performing my job since returning to work has been difficult since written communication is a key function of my role and typing with only my left hand is both slow and difficult. A letter from the Human Resources department of my company is included as Attachment C documenting my salary level and that I missed five days.

I am a competitive tennis player who regularly plays in regional competitions. My goal this year was to win the western regional competition leading to sponsorships by equipment companies. As a result of this accident, I missed the final 12 weeks of the season and will need to start down a level at the beginning of the next season, assuming I am able to play. Attachment D includes a regional ranking showing me as 12th out of 115 players in the region as well as my seeding information for the tournament I should have played in the weekend following the accident.

As a direct consequence of the negligence of your insured, I suffered great pain for several months, and missed work at a time when there was an important project underway which I should have been at work to help with. I also missed the remainder of the tennis season, eliminating me from potential sponsorships. As a result, I demand compensation for my injuries and general damages in the amount of $169,000.

You have 30 days from the receipt of this letter to respond.

Regards,

First name, last name

Sample Demand Letter - continued

In this claim, the demand amount is $169,000, which is double the amount we calculated in Chapter 4 for this serious injury example. If you recall from Chapter 4, the value of the serious injury example was roughly $84,500 and by doubling this amount, there is room to negotiate and hopefully get a final settlement around the $84,500 amount. In looking at how to increase the recovery in this example, if the sponsorships associated with playing tennis were real, more information is needed. If that income could be quantified and proven, then the demand could be greater. Without proof of this as a likely source of income, this point will not increase the value of the claim.

Finalizing the Claim

To finalize the claim, make sure the demand letter clearly indicates all reference material attached, that medical expenses are totaled properly and that your backup information for all of the important points is complete. Before sending the letter, you should have someone else read the entire package to ensure it is easy to understand that they can follow all the references to the attached materials.

Filing the Claim

With the demand letter complete and all the supporting material organized, send the entire package to the auto insurance company who is liable, or responsible, for the accident. If there is more than one party responsible, one will be designated the "primary" party. The insurance companies will let you know which party is the primary party. If you are ready to file the claim and do not know which is designated as the primary party, you should call one or both of them and ask, "Who will be the primary party?" Once the primary party is determined, send the entire package of information to the primary party by certified mail with a receipt returned to you.

Checklist of key points learned in this step:

- The demand letter is your primary opportunity to tell your side of the story, so keep it succinct and make it good.
- Get into the right state of mind by reading your notes from the time of the accident and during recovery before writing the demand letter.
- Read your medical records thoroughly to:
    - Make sure you understand them completely.
    - Ensure they are specific to the accident.
    - Identify anything an insurance company can use against you to deny your claim.
- Make sure your medical costs are complete. This total amount is a key value in determining the amount you will receive.
- Call the doctor who wrote the report and ask for an explanation of any comments in the medical records that you do not understand.
- Set a deadline for a response to the demand letter.
- Send the claims package and demand letter via certified mail with return receipt requested.

To Do:

1. _____

2. _____

3. _____

4. _____

Step 3 – Negotiating Your Claim

This section is the guide for how to negotiate your claim. The steps are the same whether negotiating with the other party's insurance company or your own.

The Demand Letter Has Been Sent: What's Next?

The next step will be to hear from a claims representative. This person may be an employee of the company or may be a contractor to the company. It is common for small or remote insurance companies to use a contractor.

The background of the claims representative varies. In larger insurance companies, the claims representative tends to be an employee of the company with little ability to influence the outcome of your claim. If you get an attorney as the claims representative, don't be intimidated. Often times, they will ask more relevant questions and may even have greater authority and autonomy in negotiating a settlement. However, in general, you should assume that whomever you are speaking with would need to get approval for the final agreement.

Before you hear back from the claims representative, make sure you are prepared to take detailed notes during each conversation with them. You will want to have clear documentation of whom you spoke with, when, what they asked and the next steps outlined in the call. Make note of their superiors' names and titles, as well as how large a settlement they can approve. You will also want to capture statements they make when explaining how their approval process works, what they have reviewed and their thoughts on a settlement. Make sure to give them specific action items to follow up on so you can monitor the progress. For example, if they express uncertainty over how to address a certain aspect of your claim, ask them to resolve this internally by a certain date and schedule a time to get an update from them on their progress.

How to Negotiate

In all likelihood, you are now months, or possibly even years, past the accident in which you were injured. It is important to realize that it is highly unlikely you will get a quick settlement. The case where an insurance company works to settle quickly is when they want to limit their liability. That time passed shortly after the accident took place. The insurance company would have already made such an offer if limiting liability were their intent. Knowing a quick settlement is out of the question, you now need to prepare for a lengthy negotiation. To ensure the negotiation will not drag on indefinitely, be sure to assign deadlines and actively manage these deadlines. The Inside Story #2 section that follows this chapter gives examples of how to do this and demonstrates the importance of assigning and tracking deadlines.

Negotiation is a process that combines establishing value (selling) for your point-of-view along with accommodating the other party's viewpoint and needs. You have started the negotiation at two-times, or double, what you believe is a fair settlement. Most likely, the other party will start the negotiation much lower than where you want to end up. Maintain your composure, even when the conversations get difficult. Through the process of negotiation, your objective is to meet somewhere in the middle.

As you enter the negotiation process with the claims representative, it is important to understand that the maximum amount you can receive at the conclusion of the negotiation is the policy limit of the insurance policy. Using the case outlined in the demand letter above, you requested $169,000 with an expectation of receiving approximately $84,500. If the insurance policy has a cap of

$50,000, then $50,000 is the maximum you will receive from the other party. To recover more money, you will need to file an additional claim (a UIM claim) against your own insurance company. Filing a UIM claim is covered in detail in step 5 of this chapter.

As the negotiation process begins, you and the insurance company are both assessing the other to determine negotiating style and whether the other party is being reasonable. From their perspective, the medical bills along with your description of injuries may leave them skeptical that your injuries are as severe as you claim. If they do not believe you (and even if they do) the approach they choose could be to let the statute of limitations expire and fight you in court. As the expiration date for the statute of limitations approaches, the insurance company may make a low-ball offer, hoping you will take it rather than fight them in court.

The negotiation begins when you send the demand letter to the insurance company. This is your opening offer that establishes the amount of money that you will settle for without going to court. As you talk through their response, you should listen for the reasons why they are skeptical your claim has the value you have assigned. You should never change the amount you requested until they give you a counter offer. Changing your request before they provide a counter offer is known as "negotiating against yourself." Don't ever negotiate against yourself. Not now, or any time in the future.

In your exchanges with the insurance company, you are basically selling your claim. You should explain why the value is what you identified in your demand letter and make sure they know you understand how to value a claim. Be sure to point out the attributes you have that make the claim stronger (discussed in Chapter 4 in the section "Valuing the Claim).

Once there is a counter offer, ask your contact for a detailed explanation on why it's low. If the reasons are specific, such as assignment of fault, or not believing the severity of the injuries, etc., address these points one at a time. When addressing these points, try to get the claims representative to agree the value is more than they included in the counter offer. If they agree, formalize this as a change in their proposal by talking with them about how this additional amount increases the value of the claim.

If you need to provide more information to increase the value of the claim, you need to find out exactly what other information would help them increase their offer. So long as this information in no way compromises your claim, you will need to provide it in some form. Always be careful not to provide additional information that they have not requested. All information you send will be reviewed carefully, and they will look for discrepancies and ways to minimize the value.

This process will continue as you work your proposals closer together. The exchange will be mostly verbal. However, with any accommodation that is made, it is recommended you document the change and send it in writing. Taking this action will make it more difficult for the other party to later deny the steps toward agreement. With each new proposal you make, convincingly explain why it is a good proposal. If this process is not making progress, ask what the limit is on the insurance policy (if you don't know that already). It is possible that the person who is responsible has a low policy limit and this is the reason they are not willing to discuss compensation in line with your expectations.

Whatever you do, do not let them bully you. Do not let them claim you do not know what you are doing. If you need to threaten back, you can threaten to file a complaint with the insurance commissioner, to hire an attorney or to speak with someone higher in the organization. If you end up speaking with someone higher in the organization, it is best to be introduced by your contact. Be gracious about how the other person has been helping you. If your contact will not make the introduction, you can call and ask for the manager of the department. Be ready and willing to follow through on any threats you make.

During the negotiation, the insurance company is likely to request information on how much money was actually paid by your medical insurance provider. They know that medical insurance companies pay a reduced, negotiated amount and they want to confuse you into believing that the claim value is based on this reduced amount as well. Do not give them this information and do not engage in this discussion with them. Only discuss the total Invoice Amounts included in your claim. If they ask you for these reduced amounts, you can simply say "I have provided you with the total medical bills, which is all you need to determine claim value, and all that I am obligated to provide."

While all negotiations shape up in different ways, it is reasonable to expect a back and forth exchange around three times. You should gradually decrease the amount of money requested with a plan to stop negotiating when you hit your bottom line. For example, if you start at $50,000 with $25,000 being an acceptable amount, following their counter offer you may go down to $35,000, then $28,000 and finally to $25,000. By making each incremental change a smaller reduction, you are sending a signal that you are nearing your minimum acceptable amount.

If you cannot get to an acceptable offer, ask how they calculated their counter offer. If a computer was used, ask them to provide you with the range the computer generated, including the high amount and the low amount. Don't accept any offer unless it is at the high end of the range. If they are not offering the high amount, you should ask for a written explanation of why not. This written explanation can be shared with an attorney and filed with insurance regulators in the form of a complaint.

Checklist of key points learned in this step:

- When presenting your settlement offer, make sure you explain in detail so the claims representative knows it is well thought out and that you have a logical basis for your demand.
- Identify what the claims representative wants when negotiating. Be sure it is a specific question. Only provide the additional information necessary to address their question, nothing else.
- Never change your demand without first receiving a counter offer.
- Only give the claims representative the Invoice Amount listed on medical bills. Do not give any information on the actual amount paid on medical bills.

To Do:

1. _____

2. _____

3. _____

4. _____

Step 4 – Settling with the Other Party

As the time period defined by the statute of limitations approaches, you will need to decide which course of action you would like to take:

- Accept the settlement amount offered.

- Hire an attorney to negotiate on your behalf and file a lawsuit if the results of the negotiation are inadequate.

- Settle with the other party's insurance company, and then file an underinsured insurance claim against your own insurance company. This option is only possible if you settled for the maximum policy limit with the other insurance company.

If you are nervous about completing the negotiation yourself, you can arrange to have an attorney lined up to consult with as you negotiate the agreement. Ask attorneys you have spoken with about the case if they would be willing to guide you in negotiating an agreement yourself. They may agree to do this in anticipation that you may ask them to complete the agreement if you get frustrated.

Using my case as an example, I found that settling with the other party's insurance company was easy. There was no argument that the other party was 100% at fault. My medical bills to date were approximately $125,000. The insurance company of the party at fault offered $50,000 to settle. This was obviously unreasonably low, but was the policy limit of the woman who hit me. Once I collected this policy limit, I then filed another claim with my own insurance company to collect the remaining money from my UIM coverage.

Note: To file a UIM claim, you need to have written proof that you reached the policy limit with your first claim. With this information, you can then file additional claims against your own policies with UIM coverage, such as your auto or umbrella policy.

Before settling, I consulted an attorney about my options. This consultation was roughly a 15-minute phone conversation. I still had not hired an attorney.

Checklist of key points learned in this step:

- Settling with an insurance company can take place:
  - At any time you believe they have made a reasonable offer, or
  - When they have made an offer equivalent to the policy limits and you do not believe a lawsuit will result in an increase in the awarded amount.
- Before settling, consult people with knowledge in the negotiation process with insurance companies. This could be an attorney or other type of specialist who has experience with how insurance companies work.
- When filing a UIM claim, make sure you have (in writing) from the other party proof of the policy limit and that you collected the full amount in your first claim.

To Do:

1. _____

2. _____

3. _____

Step 5 – Filing a Second Claim (UIM) with Your Insurer

Having successfully negotiated your first claim and having received the full policy amount, it is now time to file a second claim with your own insurance company to collect on your UIM coverage. You would file a UIM claim when:

- The responsible party's insurance policy limited the first settlement to less than the value of the claim, and

- You collected the full value of the responsible party's insurance policy, and

- You have UIM coverage with a policy limit greater than the responsible party.

For example, you filed and won a settlement of $50K with the other party's insurance company, but your total claim was $125K. You can now file a claim against your own UIM coverage to be awarded the additional $75K that you believe you are owed. The way this works is that you can recover up to the maximum amount of the largest policy. Let's say you have $100K of UIM coverage; from this amount, the $50,000 you already recovered will be deducted, meaning you can recover an additional $50,000. Similarly, if you had $125,000, or more, in UIM coverage, you could recover the full $75,000 (which is $125,000 less the $50,000 you already received.)

The following section reviews the process of updating your first claim file for a UIM claim. Most of the work in preparing the claim file was completed in Step 2 of this chapter. The additional step that follows identifies the additional work that needs to be done to file the same claim with your insurance company.

Before Filing a UIM Claim

Because you have a contract with your insurance company, you are most likely required to submit complete medical reports and work records documenting both your injures and treatments as well as time lost from work. Your policy will also specify how long you must wait for your insurance company to respond to this UIM claim before filing a lawsuit.

Whether the statute of limitations applies depends on your situation. In the case of a UM claim, the other party had no insurance so this is your first claim. In this case, the statute of limitations for your state applies. In the case of a UIM claim, this is your second claim. In this case, the statute of limitations does not apply to this second claim, but other laws governing the period of time by when a lawsuit must go to trial will likely limit the time you have. In both situations, you now have the protection of your own policy defining the timeframe when you have waited sufficiently long and can file a lawsuit.

The following will guide you through the process of updating your original claim file to include the additional documents required in your second UIM claim.

Changes to the Demand Letter

This section describes the additions you need to make to your original demand letter and claim file that you prepared in Step 2 of this Chapter.

Your Injuries and Long-term Prognosis

The written description of your injuries and long-term prognosis in the demand letter will be the same as described in Step 2 of this chapter. The difference will be in the attachments referenced. A complete file of medical reports with appropriate references in the demand letter will be needed. For example, "see Attachment A for emergency room report and description of injuries." The attachments also must include complete medical records, unless you already signed a release form allowing the insurance company to collect the information themselves.

Since the insurance company will have the complete medical file resulting from your accident (and possibly more if you did not provide the information yourself), it is imperative you make sure the file is both complete, accurate and communicates what you want to have communicated. There will be comments and terminology in these records that you may not have heard before. You will need to understand these and anticipate how the insurance company could interpret them. If the statements in these reports do not make sense to you, call your doctor and get explanations for the descriptions and terminology included in the report.

Make sure complete reports exist for each of your injuries. The report for each injury needs to include the following:

- How long were you disabled (unable to perform your work and activities of daily living)?
- Were you partially or totally disabled?
- Was the disability directly and solely a result of the accident?
- If there was a pre-existing condition, discuss with your doctor how to present such an injury to an insurance company. The doctor will know what to do in this situation and will guide you appropriately.
- What treatments were given?
- What medications were prescribed and for how long?
- What is the future outlook of your disability or pain and how much of this can be directly attributed to the accident?

Be aware that doctors and lawyers use different definitions for "probability." If there is a probability of greater than 50% of needing future treatment, have your doctor identify such treatment as probable. You will need to request your doctor to state this since doctors are not trained to think of more than 50% as "probable."

Lost Income

The written description in the demand letter will be the same as described in Step 2 of this chapter. The difference will be in the attachments referenced. The attachments will need to include documentation from your employer proving the lost income.

Deadline for a Reply

The amount of time you give for a response to your claim depends largely on the state of the medical reports you provide. If the reports have not been provided, the insurance company will need to collect them, assemble them and read through what could be an unorganized and confusing mass of paperwork. The time required to collect the reports is typically 15 to 30 days for doctors and 30 to 60 days for hospitals. Thus, if you provide all the reports, you can set a reasonable deadline for a response in 30 days. If you do not provide the medical reports, you should set a deadline for a response in 90 days to give them time to collect the reports.

If you do not provide the reports, you will find that it will not be possible to maintain any control over the schedule. For example, if the insurance company claims only partial records were received and they need to request them again, there is no way for you to know if this is true. This scenario potentially puts you into an endless delay cycle.

Setting a reasonable time limit for a response is more than just working to manage the schedule. The time limit, if ignored by the insurance company, could become an important component in your ability to win a bad faith lawsuit in the future.

If the statute of limitations applies, be certain your deadline for a reply is before the statute of limitations expires. This is the only way you can be assured of having time to prepare and file a lawsuit if the claims representative does not reply by your deadline.

Filing Your UIM Claim

The next step is the same as with all demand letters. As you did before, you should send the claims package and demand letter via certified mail with return receipt requested.

Checklist of key points learned in this step:

- The demand letter and claim file need to be updated to include:
  - Medical records
  - Work records (if there is lost income)
- Read your medical records even more thoroughly than in Step 2 since you are now definitely providing this information. Check for the following:
  - Make sure you understand the medical records completely
  - Ensure the records are specific to the accident and only the accident
  - Identify (and remove if possible) anything an insurance company can use against you to deny your claim

To Do:

1. _____

2. _____

3. _____

4. _____

5. _____

Step 6 – Negotiating and Settling with Your Insurer

The process of negotiating the settlement in a UIM claim is similar to settling with the other party's insurance company. Since you have already done it once, you are now a pro. The primary difference between the two claims is that your contract with your insurance company obligates you to provide more information, which you did in step 5, and obligates them to treat you honestly, fairly and with good faith.

It will be quickly evident if your insurance company intends to negotiate in good faith or put you into a delay cycle designed to intentionally frustrate you in an effort to minimize the value of your claim. If your insurance company enters into a good faith negotiation, refer to Step 3 – "Negotiating Your Claim" in this chapter as the guide for the negotiation process.

If your insurance company instead enters into a delay cycle, you should go along with them and keep detailed notes on every conversation. Be sure to note what the insurance company said, what they asked for, when they said certain actions would be completed, whether they completed the items they said they would, and any other stall tactics. The longer they stall, the more flagrant the violation of their obligation to treat you honestly, fairly and in good faith. Documenting that the insurance company was stalling strengthens the subsequent bad faith claim against them if you decide to pursue that later on. Make sure to keep detailed notes about their actions and how they are violating this contractual obligation. These notes could become the cornerstone of a bad faith lawsuit. To learn some of the signs of the insurance delay cycle, read The Inside Story - #2 section that follows titled "More Delays, Denials, Dishonesty and Deceit."

If the negotiation is not making progress, your options are to either accept the settlement amount offered, or file a lawsuit. Some policies may require you to go to arbitration. A discussion of the lawsuit options is included in Chapter 7.

If you believe you have a legitimate bad faith lawsuit, you should consult with an attorney on this before settling with the insurance company. When you accept an offer, a condition for getting paid will be a release of all claims against the company. This release means you give up your right to file a lawsuit in the future. You need to read the release to ensure it does not prevent you from filing a bad faith lawsuit against the company.

Checklist of key points learned in this step:

- Read your insurance policy so you know the contractual time for response to your demand letter.
- Keep detailed notes on everything the insurance company says, who said it and when. This will be your basis for proving bad faith.
- Assign action items to the claims representative during the negotiation. Whether they complete the action items will be an indicator of whether they are working to resolve the claim.
- Always maintain a deadline by which the claims representative needs to reply.
- Keep notes on whether or not the claims representative replied and the response. For example, they called back on the date specified, but talked about other points and did not address the issue.

To Do:

1. _____

2. _____

3. _____

4. _____

5. _____

The Inside Story - #2

More Delays, Denials, Dishonesty and Deceit

The Inside Story you are about to read includes more examples of intentional delays, unjustified denials, and dishonest and deceitful communications. This true story can help you recognize when the insurance company is not processing your claim, but is working to appear as if they are processing the claim.

At this point in time, I had settled with the other party's auto insurance company, which was only enough money to pay a reduced amount of the outstanding medical bills my medical insurance company refused to pay. I proceeded forward with a UIM claim with my own insurance company in an effort to recover some money for lost income and pain and suffering. After all I had been through, it seemed reasonable that an insurance policy I had been paying for in excess of twenty years should pay something from the $250,000 of UIM coverage.

According to my policy, the insurance company had 30 days to review the UIM claim file, ask questions and propose a settlement. If I was not satisfied after 30 days, I could file a lawsuit. I had provided everything they required in order to process the UIM claim. The only effort required on their part was to read the file and make a counter proposal. Based on providing all of the documentation, I gave them 15 days for the first response. My assumption was that it could take another 15 days to complete the negotiation and the process would be complete in the 30 days defined by the contract.

The following is an abridged version of the conversations I had with the claims representative.

Day 1 – The insurance company received the demand letter.

Day 14 – The demand letter had a deadline of the next day. The claims representative called and began asking questions about my "broken pelvis." I stopped her and clarified that I never had a broken pelvis. Since this was not an injury of mine, I thought she might have my claim confused with another claim. I asked if she had read the demand letter, and she assured me she had.

The only point she raised was to request more time. She wanted a time extension that was unlimited. The reason given for needing the extra time is important to note. She stated that the manager who could sign off on a claim this large would return from vacation on day 34. The claims representative said she would prepare the recommendation in advance and present it to him upon his return. This all sounded reasonable, for now. After more discussion we agreed to two points: First, the date by which they would respond to the demand letter would be rescheduled to 38 days after receipt of the letter. This was eight days more than the insurance policy stated was necessary for them to respond. Secondly, while there were no requests for additional information at this time, she promised that if such requests arose she would let me know by day 31.

Day 31 – This date came and went without any requests for additional information.

Day 36 – The claims rep called to discuss the claim. The first point she raised in the conversation was that they would need to get an economist involved. I asked her why she had not informed me of this by day 31, per our agreement. I also questioned why an economist was needed and what an economist would do. I pushed on these questions and tried to make sense of the request. Her only response was that they needed more time and she could not commit to how much more time was needed. She insisted on their response being open-ended with no date for completion.

We moved on to discuss a new point, which was medical bills and how they were used to value the claim. This was another point that should have been raised by day 31, per our agreement. She asked if information on my medical payments were included with the demand letter. Remember, this was five weeks after receiving the claim file and it appeared she still had not read the file. I pointed her to where she could find all the information on medical expenses. She said they would need to know the negotiated amounts, as they would base valuation on this, not on the full Invoice Amount of the bills.

Note: This brings up two points: a) never provide the negotiated amounts, and b) this request contradicted what another claims representative within the company told me they needed. I had the name of the person and a quote of what they said in my notes so I shared this with her.

Unable to make progress on this topic, we came back to the economist point and she said the reason for needing an economist was to assess my wage loss. I pointed out that I had included a letter from the Chief Financial Officer of my employer that detailed information about my lost wages, including time missed from work and pay rate. Therefore, there was nothing for an economist to do because there was no more information to be collected to calculate wage loss. Nevertheless, she continued to insist they needed more time due to the need for an economist.

The claim was already one week past the deadline of when the insurance company needed to make an offer, and negotiations had not even started. In fact, with each call to discuss the claim, it became more confusing. We now had claims representatives contradicting each other, requests for outside help that served no apparent purpose and requests for information to which they were not entitled. It was becoming clear that I was caught in the insurance delay cycle. The claims representative was not addressing the claim at all. I requested to speak with her supervisor so we could start moving toward closure. She denied the request and promised to quickly work the claim to closure.

As the conversation proceeded forward, I made a statement about my medical bills continuing to mount due to on-going treatment. Despite the unknown medical costs for me going forward, my desire was to settle the claim. Even though it was clearly stated in the demand letter that I was still being treated for injuries, she was surprised by this fact. At this point, the conversation changed entirely. She now claimed that the only item she needed in order to close the claim were my most recent bills and medical reports. Needless to say, I was skeptical.

I explained that the additional expenses were minimal and immaterial to the settlement. I also stated that it would take a couple of days to get the additional information and since the bills were small, resolution of the claim should not hinge on this.

Her response to this was that she would be able to use the on-going treatment as a way to get me a good settlement. She would present this, along with the rest of the information, the following Monday to the manager who would be returning from vacation. It is worth noting that this is the same person that returned from vacation one week earlier.

With regard to the point that she wanted negotiated amounts for medical bills and another claims representative had told me invoice amounts were fine, she promised to contact the other representative and resolve this issue by day 38. I was unable to gain agreement on a new deadline. Each time I pushed for a deadline, she refused to respond and became silent on the other end of the phone. If she said anything, it was only that they needed more time. After the conversation about on-going treatment, she did offer that she would propose a settlement on day 41.

Day 38 – The representative called back to check on when I would send the documents for the on-going medical treatment. I reiterated that I would send them by the next day, as promised during our last call. I took the opportunity to ask if she had closure with the other representative on why they expressed different positions. Her response was that she had not spoken with the same person, but had spoken with someone else (a person with whom I had never spoken). The two of them had concluded that I had misunderstood the earlier conversation – the conversation to which neither of them were a party. This of course was both meaningless and ridiculous since the person I had spoken with was not involved in the conversation.

She told me that if I faxed the updated medical reports by noon on day 41, she would be able to include it in the proposal for settling the claim that would take place later in the day on day 41. I faxed the documents on day 38 (as promised).

Day 41 – The communication from the claims representative was via a voicemail. In the voicemail she stated "...I respectfully request an extension, indicating that at this time I am unable to accept or reject your demand pending a review of the additional materials you submitted and applying them to your evaluation ..." Now I was certain the information she requested under the guise of needing this to get me a settlement was being used as a reason not to respond.

Six weeks of time had elapsed with the following results:

- The representative had not thoroughly read the claim.

- Not a single valid question about the claim had been raised.

- The issue that insurance company representatives had contradicted each other had not been closed. Rather than closing the issue, they had taken a bullying approach, stating that it was my fault and that I had misunderstood them (which I knew was not true based on my notes).

- The promise of a good settlement based on additional medical bills had no results. In fact, there wasn't even any discussion of a settlement.

- They continuously refused to establish deadlines.

- No partial settlement proposal had been made.

- They did not grant my request to introduce me to a supervisor.

Day 42 – I called an attorney who I had maintained contact with from early interviews, negotiated the fee agreement and hired him.

In this Inside Story section you have learned the following:

- Keep a sharp eye out for delay tactics. Illogical communication is a sign that something is wrong and an indicator they are simply stalling and not addressing the claim.
- Through the course of two claims with my own insurance company as well as claims with my medical insurance provider, I experienced dishonest and deceitful communication on so many issues.

The Attorney I Hired Played Me!

In addition to the frustration of not making progress with the insurance company, I was worried about the statute of limitations. I now had only two weeks until the two-year period lapsed. The PI attorney whom I was consulting with told me that the policy limit would not apply if my insurance company did not negotiate in good faith prior to the two-year time limit. Based on this, he offered his insight that I may be able to get "full value" for the damages. In his words, after the statute of limitations lapsed the "cap would come off the policy."

With this information from the attorney, money was now a consideration. The long-term effects of the accident were much more than I had ever imagined. On top of this, the difficulties of dealing with the insurance company were simply unacceptable. The option of recovering nearly three times as much by hiring an attorney was an easy decision. I finalized negotiation of the contract with the attorney and signed him on as my legal counsel.

The next step (or lack thereof) came as quite a surprise. The attorney did nothing. He did not file a lawsuit before the two-year time period lapsed. When I asked him directly about this, he claimed he had misinterpreted the law and that the statute of limitations only applied to the first party, not my own UIM policy. This is basic information a lawyer needs to understand in order to effectively practice his chosen profession. While he did not admit this to me, I believe he was fully aware of what the truth was, even while he was telling me exactly the opposite. The attorney's greed had motivated him to be dishonest in order to sign me as a client.

In this Inside Story section you have learned the following:

- Don't trust anyone who wants your business.
- Always get a second opinion.

Chapter 7 – Lawsuits: Small Claims vs. Arbitration vs. Court

If you aren't having any success settling your claim, the time has come to get a third party involved that can impose a deadline and force a decision. There are three options available:

Small claims court

An independent arbitrator

Litigating through the court system

This chapter includes a discussion of each approach and helps you decide which best applies to your situation.

Small Claims Court

Small claims court is intended for resolving small monetary issues without the need for an attorney. Some states even forbid attorneys in small claims court. The state you live in will have a guide that tells you if your claim amount is small enough to file a lawsuit in small claims court. Check Appendix F of this book, or the State Laws page of the Injured Money website, www.injuredmoney.com, for the small claims court dollar amount limit in your state.

The small claims court will provide the forms needed to formally file a lawsuit. The preparation you have done collecting documents, getting witness statements and calculating injury value is the information you need to present your case. Assuming you were thorough in preparing the claim sent to the insurance company, you do not need an attorney.

Court procedures will vary from state to state, so check with the court in your state to become familiar with their procedures. The Laws by State section of the website www.injuredmoney.com provides a link to small claims court information for your state. Use this link, or a search engine, to help find the information you need. You should also be certain to download the required forms for filing the complaint and bring a copy of the demand letter and all supporting documentation to the courthouse. Eyewitnesses can be invited to talk on your behalf.

To prepare for presenting your case, you should attend a small claims court hearing in advance of your court date. This will enable you to watch the proceedings and make notes of what you should and should not do in order to win your own case. You can then go home and rehearse your presentation until you feel comfortable that you can make a convincing verbal argument. How convincingly you present your case will have a significant influence on who wins.

Arbitration

Arbitration has a similar informality as small claims court, but without the dollar limit on the claim amount. If the claim is against your own insurance company, your policy may dictate that you go to arbitration. Check your insurance policy to determine if arbitration is the route you must choose when contesting a claim against your insurance company.

The advantages of arbitration are that it is simple and informal, so you may be able to represent yourself and not have an attorney. Also, the process is likely to be quicker than the court system. The disadvantage of arbitration is that the outcome is often binding, meaning if you lose, you have no ability to appeal the decision.

In general, insurance companies prefer arbitration over going to court, primarily because insurance companies believe the likelihood of large settlements awarded by juries is low with arbitration. There is also the motivation that settlements in arbitration do not become publicly available. This helps insurance companies keep any information about settlements they have paid out of the public eye.

While it is possible to represent yourself in arbitration, it is not recommended. The main reason is that part of the arbitration process is agreeing to a mutually acceptable arbitrator. As a layman, you don't know which arbitrators may be sympathetic to you, the policyholder or the insurance company. A good lawyer will know this information and be able to effectively negotiate for the right arbitrator.

Once arbitration is complete, the arbitrator should render the final decision within 30 days. As stated above, arbitration is often "binding," meaning you have no recourse to appeal the decision made.

The Court System

The court system, while effective, is highly technical. This book does not offer advice on representing yourself in a lawsuit tried in the court system. If you have reached this point, it is recommended you hire an attorney to guide you through the judicial process.

The Attorney's Role, for Arbitration or Trial

If you decide to hire an attorney for arbitration or trial, you should still have written a draft demand letter and gathered supporting documentation. The attorney will take care of filing a lawsuit or a petition for arbitration, negotiate for a mutually acceptable arbitrator (if arbitration is the route taken), schedule the necessary depositions and schedule the hearing. Depositions are an important part of the process where key people such as medical experts, witnesses or others with information or expertise that impacts the case give testimony under oath. Depositions are part of the preparation process and are taken in advance of the hearing or trial.

Before the hearing, you and your attorney will need to have a detailed pre-meeting to discuss all points of the demand, key facts supporting your claim and how to address points you expect the defense (the insurance company) to raise. Be sure to review all the Other Factors from Chapter 4 so you are prepared to present the positive factors, and address the negative factors the insurance company will raise about you. Both you and the attorney will need to attend the hearing or trial. How convincingly your case is presented will have a significant influence on the outcome.

Keep in mind, however, that hiring an attorney does not mean you will get a quick settlement. In my case, the negotiation over whom to use as the arbitrator began three months after hiring the attorney and concluded one month later. It then took nearly four months to find a date when the arbitrator, my lawyer, the insurance company's lawyer and I were available for the arbitration hearing. In total, I waited eight months from the time I hired an attorney until the arbitration hearing. If your case goes to court rather than arbitration, you should expect the time required to be even greater.

During the intervening time between filing the suit and a hearing, there will be an exchange of information between your lawyer and the insurance company's lawyers. This information will be in the form of questions designed to help both sides build their case and prepare for defending the case. For me, my case was clear. The police had assigned fault to the other driver, my medical bills were over $125,000, all the required reports were submitted and the demand was clear. There wasn't any additional information we needed to collect.

The insurance company's case, on the other hand, had not been established at all. They knew that in order to win the arbitration process, they needed to present reasons why my insurance policy did not apply and they didn't owe me money. My expectation was that once the lawsuit was filed, the insurance company would begin seriously working to understand the claim. But there were no requests for information, just silence.

The silence was broken a month after scheduling the date for hearing, which was nearly five months after hiring an attorney and three months before we were scheduled to go in front of the arbitrator. The insurance company's request was to depose the doctor who performed the hip surgery.

> *Note*: The timeline is described above to emphasize the point that the insurance company wants to delay paying you as long as possible. The insurance company benefits from this delay in two ways: First, they continue to earn investment income off of your money invested for their benefit, and second, as time passes, your frustration continues to grow and creates a willingness on your part to settle for less so you can end the frustration.

Checklist of key points learned in this chapter:

- When the dollar amount of your claim is equal to or less than the limit of your state's small claims court, this is an option for settling the claim with minimal cost.
- Negotiating for an arbitrator who is sympathetic to policyholders and managing the process necessitates an attorney for arbitration.
- Always rehearse your answers to questions and statements you want to make before going to a hearing.
- To maximize your financial recovery, you must be prepared for a lengthy process.

To Do:

1. _____

2. _____

3. _____

4. _____

The Inside Story - #3

The Insurance Company's Attorney Modified my Medical Records

Five months after ending direct negotiation with my insurance company, they requested to depose (take testimony under oath) my hip doctor. It was during this deposition that I found out the insurance company's attorney had modified my medical records. During the deposition, they presented my doctor with their falsified information and suggested to him that the cause of my hip problems were events other than the accident.

Included below are excerpts from the deposition where my insurance company's attorney presented the falsified information. This is included to give you an appreciation of both the deposition process and the underhandedness of the insurance companies and their representatives:

> **Attorney:** *Do you know if Mr. Karr had ridden a bicycle between June 2007 (the date of the accident) and the date of your surgery in May 2008?*
>
> **Doctor***: I don't know specifically. I know he loves to bike, but I don't know if he rode in-between. Let me see. If it's not in my note(s), I wouldn't know. Let me see if I put down in my note anything to that effect. Let's see. Yeah. He tried going back to biking but it hurt him a lot. He obviously tried. So that's the answer.*
>
> **Attorney***: For example, what I found in reading (was that) Optometric Center... On May 27, '08 it indicates*

that he told them he had gone on a death ride (which is a big ride in the California mountains) that year. And I think from other cases, death rides, these guys run up and down mountains on bicycles and stuff.

Doctor: *Well, I know the death ride as being the Markleeville Death Ride, which is a total of 15,000 vertical feet of climbing and about 150 miles of bike riding.*

Attorney: *Isn't that hard on your joints?*

Doctor: *I think it's harder on your lungs.*

Attorney: *Oh.*

Doctor: *Yeah. I mean I wouldn't be able to do it at this point in my life.*

Attorney: *I wondered: Would that bicycling doing things like the death ride **prior to his surgery with you have exacerbated this condition post injury?** What would it have done? What would it have made worse? Would it have resulted in more formation of tissue?*

In the transcript above, the auto insurance company's attorney modified my medical records to make it appear as if I had ridden in the Death Ride in the weeks following my accident, when in fact I was in bed recovering from serious injuries. The reality was that I rode in this bicycle ride the year before my accident occurred and that bit of information had been included in my eye doctor's notes from a past yearly eye exam. I must have mentioned this bike ride to my doctor in conversation and never realized he would have included this in his notes since it had nothing to do with my eyes. However, the insurance company's attorney poured over my records, found this note and proceeded to change the date to make it look as if I had ridden in this challenging ride shortly after my accident.

Fortunately for me, my hip doctor proceeded to explain that independent of all other events, before or after the surgery, the accident had caused damage to my hip that he expected would result in the need for a replacement hip in the future. This was the only fact that mattered and is what settled the case. Had he questioned his conviction based on their false and misleading accusations, the outcome may have been very different. Because I was not in the deposition, I was not there to defend myself and tell the doctor that I had not ridden this bike ride right after my accident. Another doctor may have believed their lies and changed his opinion based on this falsified information.

> *Note*: In Chapter 2 we discussed that not all doctors will offer an opinion. In fact, some hospitals have a policy that their doctors cannot offer an opinion. They will only comment on what they did and what they saw during diagnosis and surgery. Had I proceeded with the surgery by my first hip doctor (who had a policy against offering opinions), I may well have lost this case.

Following this deposition with my hip doctor and five days prior to our scheduled arbitration, my insurance company then initiated a frantic process of paying me the full policy value for my UIM coverage. Because I had hired an attorney to recover this money, the check for the full amount was written to my attorney. The attorney then deducted his fees and paid me the remaining award amount. The policy limit of my insurance policy had now been collected, so there was no more money to recover based on the insurance claim.

This is of course, unjust. An attorney should not have been necessary, and the payment of the award should have occurred long before this date. This is the unfortunate reality of how the system currently works. Recovering the damages from an unjust system, as was just been described, is covered in Chapter 9 – Insurance Bad Faith.

In this Inside Story section, you have witnessed the following:

- The insurance company never presented a single legitimate reason for delaying or denying either of my claims. This is unfortunately how they work and what is currently permissible under the laws and regulations governing insurance.
- You must be aggressive and diligent in order to recover what is rightfully yours.

Maximizing $$$s, Minimizing Attorney's Fees

PI lawyers are typically paid on a contingency fee, which means they only get paid if they win your case. As a result, attorneys want to invest the least amount of time necessary to win your case. While most people think they need a lawyer to proceed with any claim, the reality is that you may be able to save considerable money by handling parts, or all, of your claim yourself. In my case, I was able to completely manage and settle my first claim with the other party's insurance company and I handled the preparation work for the second claim. This saved me $40,500 in attorney's fees between the preparation I did and the claims in which I represented myself.

For my second claim, I decided to hire a PI attorney because the claim had been caught in the insurance company's deliberate delay cycle. I needed legal help to push this second claim through the system and this required an attorney to file a lawsuit on my behalf. However, even though I hired an attorney, the preparation I had done for my case enabled me to reduce the contingency fee for the attorney from the typical 33%

down to 25%. That is why it is so important to make sure you keep yourself organized as we covered in Chapter 2.

As you can see, there are many opportunities for you to handle all, or parts, of your claim without having to hire a lawyer. Below is a summary of how I maximized my compensation:

- I settled my first claim with the other party's insurance company without hiring a lawyer.

- I negotiated and settled seven independent agreements with medical providers to reduce what I owed them (discussed in Chapter 5).

- I prepared my own claim and negotiated with my insurance company long enough to enable me to reduce the attorney's rate from 33% to 25%.

- You can save significant money by being selective about when to use an attorney. However, don't miss an opportunity for a larger settlement by not using an attorney.

Chapter 8 – Attorneys: Hiring, Compensating and Managing

The primary objective throughout the claims process is to get a fair compensation for your pain and suffering, lost income and lost opportunities as a consequence of your injuries. This book has explained how to calculate the amount that represents a fair recovery. The challenge that remains is that you may not know if you can recover this compensation by yourself, or if you will need the professional assistance of an attorney. If you are far along in the process, your patience may be wearing thin and the statute of limitations may be rapidly approaching. You will likely feel like you are being pushed into a corner with no escape route. Beware: working you into a corner is the insurance company's objective.

To avoid the scenario where your financial recovery becomes worthless, you should consult with attorneys early in the process so that they are on hand to step in if you need them at some point. Most likely, it will not be evident if you need an attorney until just before the statute of limitations lapses. When it finally becomes evident that an attorney is needed, you will need to act quickly. The preliminary work you've done to contact attorneys and discuss your claim puts you in a position to hire an attorney on short notice.

To Hire or Not to Hire?

This section helps you determine whether it is time for you to hire an attorney. The first step is to understand where you are in the process and what your options are. The simple description is: if it appears as if you will file a lawsuit (not prosecuted in small claims court), then an attorney is necessary. The table that follows is a more detailed guide for determining whether it is time to hire an attorney to represent you.

Table 7: Conditions for deciding when to hire an attorney.

	Situation: Should you to hire an attorney now?	Yes	Not yet necessary
1	Are you early in the process and willing to do the preparation for the case?		✓
2	If your claim goes to court, will it go to small claims court? For dollar limits on small claims court check Appendix F.		✓
3	Have you done the homework to know if your small claims court lawsuit qualifies for double or treble damages? If you do not have an understanding of this, you should at least consult with an attorney to get guidance, but still should not need an attorney to represent you in small claims court.		✓
4	Are you confident you understand how the statute of limitations affects your claim and are comfortable filing and negotiating the claim yourself?		✓
5	Have you given the insurance company adequate time to respond, but haven't been able to get a reasonable offer? Your insurance company policy may require you to go to arbitration for which you can represent yourself. However, this book recommends hiring an attorney.	✓	✓
6	Have you given the insurance company adequate time to respond, but haven't been able to get a reasonable offer? You plan to litigate in a court of law.	✓	

	Situation: Should you to hire an attorney now?	Yes	Not yet necessary
7	Are you fixated on receiving the largest possible settlement and unwilling to accept anything less?	✓	
8	Has the insurance company accused you of fraud and sent your claim to a fraud investigation team?	✓	

At any point along the way, if you are not comfortable and confident in your ability to successfully recover the damages you are owed, then hiring an attorney is advised.

The Hiring Process

There are four key points to address in order to hire the right attorney:

1. You need to find an attorney with whom you are compatible.

   Hiring an attorney is similar to hiring an employee. Once hired, you will need to spend time talking with him and discussing the details of your case. There may be times when you will not be present, so it is essential that you trust your attorney to represent you the way you want to be represented.

   One way to identify an attorney is to ask your doctors if they know PI attorneys who they trust and personally like. If your doctor has been involved in personal injury claims before, he has likely been deposed or given testimony under oath by an attorney. Your doctors will know which attorneys have done a good job representing their clients and stand out as top performers. Once you meet the attorney, you will want to understand how organized he is, if his communication style is compatible with yours and whether you like working with him, etc.

2. The attorney should have experience working with the insurance company with which you are dealing – and he should have a track record of winning cases against them.

    The key to winning negotiations is knowing the organization and people with whom you are negotiating. If the attorney knows the insurance company you are dealing with, he will know the culture of the company and how they have historically behaved in negotiations.

    During the claims process, there are a large number of claims representatives within the large insurance companies, so knowing the claims representatives is unlikely. When the claim moves to a lawsuit, the people involved from the insurance company's side is narrowed down. Typically, the insurance company has a small number of attorneys who are employees supported by outside contractors, who are also attorneys, who represent the company. Having an attorney who has dealt with these people before will help you anticipate their next move and have an idea of what they are willing to settle for without going to court.

3. Your attorney needs to explain the technicalities of the law and justice system accurately and in a way that you understand. Ask the attorneys you interview about the laws that apply to your situation, the options for how to prosecute the case, the risks and rewards of these options and their recommendations. From this interview process, you can learn a significant amount and you will get a feel for whether you can easily communicate with this attorney.

    When you are still in the interview phase, you should check any facts that the attorney tells you to make sure they are accurate and truthful. If you suspect they are not truthful, you should find another attorney.

4. If possible, your attorney should have experience with a case like yours.

However, it is more important that your attorney has experience settling claims against the same insurance company, so if he only has this experience and not with your particular type of case, he still might be the right choice. The reason for this is that it's more important to know the people and company with whom you are negotiating than the type of accident. Try to get a lawyer who has both types of experience but if you cannot, go with the one who has worked with your insurance company in the past.

Before actually signing a contingency fee agreement with an attorney, you should check his professional references. The attorney should provide references you can check as part of the selection process. Ask for a list of cases he has settled, preferably with the same insurance company. Make a list of questions to ask the references and contact all of them. Be diligent about asking all your questions and listen carefully. Even positive references can give you insight into personality quirks. Make sure the references are other clients, and not other attorneys.

Compensating

Personal Injury and Insurance bad faith (covered in Chapter 9) lawyers typically work on a contingency fee plus out-of-pocket expenses. The definition of a contingency fee is "no win, no fee." If you don't win, they get nothing. The advantage of having a contingency fee agreement with your attorney is that you don't have to come up with the money out of your pocket to pay him. The disadvantage is that the attorney may achieve the best return on his invested time by settling easily, with less time and effort, for less money. It can be difficult to determine if this is his motivation.

If you are having difficulty getting a good attorney interested in your case, you should ask the attorney why he isn't interested and you may need to re-evaluate whether you have a valid claim.

Contingency fees are based on a percentage of the total award in the case. The percentage can be as low as 25%, but is typically 33% if the dispute is settled out of court and before the serious preparation for the court appearance begins. When your case goes to court, the contingency fee increases to a typical rate of 40% because there is more work involved. On top of this fee, you will also need to pay out-of-pocket expenses such as hiring an expert witness to provide an opinion on the case. The attorney will pay these fees up front and you will need to reimburse him after you receive your settlement.

The reason the fees increase to roughly 40% when going to court is because the preparation involved and the time required for a court appearance are significant. The attorney will need to invest both time and money paying for the depositions and questioning of expert witnesses and key people on the other side of the case to help build a strong case.

While arbitration and mediation are a more formal process than simply negotiating a claim, they should not be viewed as "going to court." These processes are much less involved and do not justify an increase in fees.

Therefore, you should carefully negotiate the wording in the attorney contract on when the increase to 40% would take place. Filing the lawsuit is simply turning in the proper paperwork with the courts. The additional work that would justify higher fees does not begin until the court date has been scheduled. Make sure your contract clearly states that any increase in fees will not take place until a specific number of days prior to the court date as opposed to when the lawsuit is filed.

Also, if you were referred to the attorney by another attorney, it is customary for attorneys to pay a referral fee to the attorney who refers you to him. This fee is a pre-determined percentage of the total fees. Make sure this referral fee does not impact the percentage you are charged. The referral is between the attorneys and should have no impact on your fee arrangement.

As you finalize a contract with an attorney, keep in mind that it is possible to negotiate a reduction in fees. In my case, I minimized the total legal fees by finalizing several agreements without an attorney. I further reduced the legal fee by negotiating the normal 33% rate down to 25% for the first $200,000 recovered. To make sure there was incentive to recover as much money as possible, I agreed to increase the fee back up to 33% on any amount greater than $200,000.

It is unlikely that you will get the fee below 25%. Be careful to consider that if you negotiate too hard on the fee, the attorney may not accept your case. Also, an attorney who is willing to take an exceptionally low rate may not have much business. If the reason he doesn't have much business is because he's not a great attorney, then getting a lower fee could cost you money in the end through a smaller settlement.

Make sure the fee agreement is specific on what the fees will cover. For example, if you have already recovered money on your own, make sure it is excluded from the fee agreement. Also, if there is potential for additional, but separate cases, such as a bad faith lawsuit, you should exclude any future cases from the agreement. Future cases may need to be handled by an attorney with different expertise, so you do not want to be contractually committed to the PI attorney as the case moves forward.

You should discuss the estimated out-of-pocket costs with your attorney prior to signing a contract. The cost of obtaining records, filing court orders, messenger service, copying, traveling, etc. should be minimal. In my case, the costs were just under $1,000. These costs can go up significantly if you have a complicated case that requires your side to hire expert witnesses to be questioned in front of a judge, jury, arbitrator or mediator.

Carefully review any document prior to signing and be sure that you fully understand the compensation. As part of the compensation, you should do the math to figure out what the attorney will cost and make sure you are ending up with more money than you would without an attorney. The following is an example of this math, assuming you agreed to pay the standard 33% lawyer fee:

In this example, we will assume that you have not yet hired a lawyer and your insurance company has offered to pay you $25,000. If you accept the offer, you keep all $25,000 because you have no legal fees. However, if the insurance policy is worth $50,000 and an attorney can get you the full $50,000, you end up with more money by hiring a lawyer. This calculation is done as follows:

- Figure out how much you would have to pay a lawyer. In this example, if you were awarded $50,000 and had to pay your attorney 33% of that, that means your lawyer would get $16,500.

$50,000 X 33% = $16,500

- Next, figure out how much you would have left over for yourself after paying lawyer fees. Using this same example, if you were awarded $50,000 and had to pay an attorney $16,500 of that, you would have $33,500 remaining for yourself.

$50,000 - $16,500 = $33,500

- Find out if there are any hard costs, such as paid depositions, that you would have to pay the lawyer and subtract those from the $33,500.

In this example above, you would get more money if you hired a lawyer and, as a result, were able to get the full policy amount of $50,000.

There is also another factor to consider, which is how long the process will take with and without an attorney. You will need to decide whether you are willing to wait a longer period of time to get more money. Filing a lawsuit often delays the settlement and does not necessarily mean you will get more money.

If the fee agreement is complicated and difficult to understand, there is something wrong. Find a different attorney.

Managing

If you decide to hire an attorney, then the section titled "Preparation: Enabling You to Win Your Claim" in Chapter 2 still applies to you and is a critical step you must undertake. Items such as summarizing your medical bills, keeping detailed notes and drafting the demand letter are essential to winning an auto insurance claim. You are the only person who knows exactly what took place and can accurately relay everything you experienced. To win, you need to be involved enough that you can give your attorney the information he needs to win on your behalf.

Checklist of key points learned in this chapter:

- The key criteria in selecting an attorney are:
  - Find an attorney with whom you are compatible.
  - The attorney should have a track record of winning cases against the insurance company with which you are dealing.
  - The attorney needs to explain the technicalities of the law and justice system both accurately and in a way that you understand.
- If possible, experience with a case like yours is preferred.
- Don't pay a PI attorney by the hour.
- Carefully review the wording describing when the contingency fee percentage increases if a lawsuit is filed.

To Do:

1. _____

2. _____

3. _____

4. _____

Chapter 9 – Insurance Bad Faith

Bad faith is the improper denial of insurance claims. When buying insurance, the policyholder pays the premium in exchange for the promise of insurance. The insurance company in return owes the policyholder a duty of good faith and fair dealing. This faith of good duty is violated when the insurance company does not respond to requests to settle or works to intentionally delay the process in order to keep the money and frustrate the claimant. If you are having difficulty collecting an insurance claim, there is a possibility that you have a justified "bad faith" claim against your insurance company.

Bad faith lawsuits are primarily against your own insurance company because you have a contract with them and they are legally required to act fairly and in good faith. The other party's insurance company used to also have a faith of duty toward an injured person, but the powerful lobbying efforts of the insurance industry has made it nearly impossible to bring a lawsuit against another parties insurance company.

The attorney who prosecutes a bad faith lawsuit may also be a PI attorney, but needs to have a specialty in bad faith law. As with PI, you want an attorney who knows the case law for their specialty inside and out. It may be beneficial if your attorney knows the attorneys from the insurance company since this will provide familiarity with the negotiation process and better insight into what may be achievable as the final settlement.

The Components of Bad Faith

In a bad faith case, there are four categories where penalties can be applied:

- Recovery of money, plus interest, which was rightfully yours but you lost the use of because it was not paid in a timely manner. An example of this would be if your insurance company delayed the claim by an unreasonable amount of time and forced you to hire an attorney to recover the money. You would be eligible to receive interest on that money you should have received and also get reimbursed for any lawyer fees, plus interest, that were necessary in order to collect the claim.

- Emotional distress. The insurance company has a legal duty to use reasonable care to avoid causing you emotional distress. If they cause you emotional distress, you can potentially be compensated. However, an insurance company will rigorously fight to not pay any amount as emotional distress, unless they are ordered to in a jury trial. Winning this point with a jury will depend heavily on the judge, the court system and the jury selected.

- Punitive damages. If the insurance company knowingly acted in a contemptible fashion, you may be eligible for receiving punitive damages. This is a category in which very large settlements can be realized, but can be very difficult proving in a court of law. You should consult with attorneys to assess whether the legal system in your state may be inclined to award punitive damages, but be sure to assess your probability well before risking the time and expense associated with a trial.

- Recovery of attorney fees for the bad faith case. There are attorney fees for the bad faith case in addition to the attorney fees you are working to recover for the PI case. The objective for the bad faith case is to get enough money that you recover all of the three items above as well as the attorneys' fees for the bad faith lawsuit.

Let's use an example scenario to calculate the potential compensation you could get from a bad faith lawsuit. For the following example, let's assume an interest rate of 10% per year.

Late payment: If it took the insurance company one year to pay you $20,000, then you are eligible to receive approximately $2,000 in interest:

TOTAL PAYMENT X 10% ANNUAL INTEREST RATE = TOTAL INTEREST

$20,000 X 10% = $2,000

Lawyer's fees: If you were forced to hire a lawyer and had to pay him/her 33% of your final $20,000 settlement, then you are eligible to be reimbursed for these legal fees. That means the insurance company would pay you back the $6,600 that you had to pay the lawyer in order to finalize the claim in a timely manner.

TOTAL PAYMENT X ATTORNEY'S PERCENTAGE = TOTAL ATTORNEY'S FEE

$20,000 X 33% = $6,600

Interest on attorney fees: Let's assume it took an additional year to recover the legal fees of $6,600. That means the insurance company would owe you 10% interest, or $660, on this money that you should have received a year ago.

TOTAL ATTORNEY'S FEE X 10% ANNUAL INTEREST RATE = INTEREST ON ATTORNEY'S FEE

($6,600 X 10%) = $660

For this example, based on looking only at the recovery of money plus interest, it is reasonable to expect to recover the $9,260 that was rightfully yours but was denied due to the bad faith of the insurance company:

$2,000 (INTEREST) + $6,600 (ATTORNEY'S FEES) + $660 (INTEREST ON ATTORNEY'S FEES) = $9,260.

In addition to the recovery of money, plus interest, you lost the use of you may be able to recover money for emotional stress, punitive damages and the attorney's fees for the bad faith lawsuit. Estimating these amounts depends on the specifics of your lawsuit and the court system in which the case would be tried. To add these additional amounts to the recovery of money you lost use of, contact a bad faith attorney.

Insurance companies attempt to settle bad faith cases in an amount slightly more than what you should have had if no attorneys or lawsuits were necessary. Their objective is to be vague about how the amount was arrived at to avoid people finding out they were subject to punitive damages or emotional stress.

Checklist of key points learned in this chapter:

- You have a legitimate bad faith case if the insurance company is not responding to your request to settle, working to intentionally delay the process to keep your money and deliberately frustrate you, or even twisting the truth (lying) in an attempt to destroy your credibility.
- Hire an attorney with specialty in the litigation of insurance bad faith.

To Do:

1. _____

2. _____

3. _____

Chapter 10 – Why Insurance Companies Stopped Providing Insurance

According to J.D. Power Associates, only 5% of insurance policyholders who held homeowner's and auto insurance with the same company changed insurance companies during 2011. Said another way, people who own bundled auto and homeowner's insurance switch carriers on average of only once every 20 years. Using 20 years as the average period of time an owner of auto and homeowner's insurance stays with one carrier, let's look at how the insurance products sold changed over a twenty-year period of time.

Profits Dramatically Increased by Not Paying Claims

One way to measure whether the auto and homeowner's insurance industry has honored their promise to provide insurance to policyholders is to review trends in the "pure loss ratio." Pure loss ratio compares how many dollars insurance companies paid out to policyholders for claims versus how many dollars they collected in premiums from their policyholders.

Chart 1: Pure Loss Ratio for Homeowners and Auto Insurance Companies.

The chart above shows that over a 20-year period, the homeowners and auto insurance industry reduced the amount they paid in claims by $0.11 for every dollar they collected in premiums. This means that in 2007 insurance companies were paying 16% less than they paid in 1987. In other words, for every dollar that policy holders (like you and I) paid to insurance companies, only $0.56 was actually returned to policyholders in the form of claims paid.[1] In essence, the insurance companies kept half the money they collected from their customers.

Systematic Defrauding of Consumers

Led by business consulting firms in the early 1990s, several large insurers began a process of changing, or as they called it, re-engineering, the claims process and viewing it as a profit center. Through this re-engineering, the industry quietly re-defined the payment claimants would receive. This re-definition included:

- Creating incentive programs designed to reduce the average payout of claims.[2]

- Preventing adjusters from being able to approve payments more than the computer calculated payment amount.[3]

- Providing incentives to claims representatives for having a low rate of claims in which an attorney represents the claimant.[4]

- Increasing the difficulty for consumers to settle claims by establishing a pre-determined percentage of claims to close without payment.[5]

- Increasing the number of policyholders referred to fraud investigation.[6]

- Forcing more policyholders to file lawsuits in order to receive what they are owed.[7]

- Eliminating entire categories of claims, such as soft tissue damage, by aggressively defending claims in order to discourage attorneys from representing consumers in these types of claims.[8]

In short, auto and homeowner's insurance policies no longer provide the protection they used to. This problem began in the early 1990's and to date, continues to become an increasingly serious problem.

The Chairman of Allstate, Jerry Choate, described the industry-wide effort to reduce what insurance companies paid in claims in order to increase profits in 1997 when he said, "In the long run, if we don't win on the claim side of this business, we don't win. Because that's where all the leverage is. Three-quarters of every dollar that leaves this company goes to pay claims. So we have to build a long-term, sustainable advantage in claims. It's as simple as that."

One the easiest ways insurance companies instituted a system of underpaying claims was through the adoption of computer programs. With the intent to reduce claims payment already in place, computer programs facilitated the implementation of the change. The most well-known computer programs includes one from Computer Science

Corporation (CSC) known as "Colossus" and another from the Insurance Services Organization known as "Claims Outcome Advisor." These programs provided the ability to dial in the savings desired for claims payments. The sales literature from CSC touted Colossus as "the most powerful cost savings tool" and suggested that the program would immediately reduce the size of bodily injury claims by up to 20 percent.

As reported in the book "From Good Hands to Boxing Gloves – How Allstate Changed Casualty Insurance in America[9]," "any insurer who buys a license to use Colossus is able to calibrate the amount of 'savings' it wants Colossus to generate...If Colossus does not generate sufficient 'savings' to meet the insurer's needs or goals, the insurer simply goes back and 'adjusts' the benchmark values until Colossus produces the desired results."

Illegitimate Profits

In the U.S., the property-casualty insurance industry collects approximately $450 billion annually in insurance premiums. Saving $0.11 cents on every dollar equates to additional profits of $49.5 billion per year.

Based on their own analysis, the Consumer Federation of America summarizes the impact of programs such as Colossus saying they "are designed to systematically underpay policyholders without adequately examining the validity of each individual claim. The use of these programs severs the promise of good faith that insurers owe to their policyholders. Any increase in profits cannot be considered legitimate."[10]

Consumers Don't Realize... Until It's Too Late

Most insurance claims are minor events such as fender benders or a fence blown down in a storm. Insurance companies readily pay these small claims, creating good will in the process. But reality is, these claims are inconveniences, not calamities. Insurance against inconvenience is nice, but insurance covering catastrophe is necessary.

Unfortunately, consumers do not realize that they are paying for insurance, but are not insured against the calamity. This brutal reality will not be learned until it is too late, after consumers like you and I have suffered a serious accident or loss.

Chapter 11 – What Consumers (You) Can Do

The systematic defrauding of policyholders by insurance companies is a serious problem that urgently needs to be addressed. In the past, consumers have relied on state government and regulatory bodies for protection. Fortunately, waiting for action by legislative bodies and regulatory commissions is no longer consumers' only option.

In the age of the Internet, consumers have the ability to join together, to learn from each other so that we all know which insurance companies we can trust with our business. The Injured Money website, www.injuredmoney.com, is dedicated to creating a communication channel where consumers can share information and learn which insurance companies pay claims.

The following information about insurance companies is available on the Injured Money website:

- Independent publications rating insurance companies.

- The Injured Money Rating System measures how good insurance companies are at paying claims. The system is based on published financial information reported by insurance companies. This industry standard rating system enables people to determine the quality of the insurance offered by insurance companies.

The best way for consumers to know which insurance companies pay claims is through all of us sharing information so everyone knows where to find help and where to learn which insurance companies are deserving of your business. To do this, we must let our friends and family know that advocacy groups like Injured Money, LLC are working diligently to help all consumers. To spread this message, use your favorite social networking site to share the story. Help others by sharing Injured Money on Facebook, Twitter, Google +, Instagram, LinkedIn, Pinterest, Digg, StumblUpon, Tumblr, Reddit, etc.

In addition to spreading this information through social media, you can follow the steps listed below under "consumers" to help protect yourself against buying insurance from a company that does not have a history of honoring their promise to pay claims. Also, contact your government officials and demand legislative reform and better regulatory oversight in the insurance industry. Contact local state officials (congressmen, senators, insurance commissioners, etc.) and let them know that policyholders depend on them to do the right thing. Take the actions listed below under the sections for both federal and state governments.

Consumers:

- Protect yourself by actively shopping for an insurance company based on the Injured Money Rating System. This system helps you understand how good insurance companies are at paying claims based on an analysis of their published financial information. Insurance companies with financial metrics earning them a rating of ★★★★★ or

  ★★★★☆ are the best in paying policyholders' claims. Fewer stars in the rating means the company is less efficient at providing insurance than other companies or they keep your insurance dollars to increase their profits. The Injured Money website will be providing a service based on this rating system so you can find out how good your insurance company is at paying claims.

- Carefully review your policies to understand coverage, out-of-pocket costs and when and how claims payments are triggered.

- When you experience problems with insurance companies, file a complaint with the state insurance commissioner.

Federal Government – legislative changes needed:

- Demand your Representatives and Senators in Washington D.C. repeal the McCarran-Ferguson Act's antitrust exemption for insurance companies. This act results in abuses that hurt consumers directly as well as the overall economy. Examples of such abuses include collusion through advisory organizations such as the Insurance Services Office (ISO) that develops and files with the state's large portions of the rates schedules.

State Governments – demand your state government's legislature and insurance commissioners institute laws and regulations that:

- Increase the oversight of computer-based claims settlement procedures. The use of computer programs has shielded insurers from necessary scrutiny and oversight of their claims practices. Understanding and regulating how claims are valued and settled is mandatory to ensure insurance companies are delivering on the promise of insurance "to assume the risk and provide prompt and fair compensation to the policyholder in the event of a loss."

- Clarify bad faith laws defining the standard for being treated reasonably and fairly. This clarification enables more policyholders to bring bad faith lawsuits against insurance companies.

- Published data measuring the treatment of consumers through their claim handling performance needs to be shared publicly and easily accessible. This data is being collected by the National Association of Insurance Commissioners (NAIC) but not shared with the public due to insistence by insurance companies that the data is proprietary.

- Adopt the NAIC's Model Unfair Claims Settlement Practices Act covering both types of claimants (policyholders and non-policyholders). The act adopted further needs to have penalties and fines of a magnitude that discourages companies from reprehensible behavior.

When making an insurance claim, don't give up. Fight for what is rightfully yours.

Thank you for reading my book. If you enjoyed it, please take a moment to leave me a review at your favorite retailer.

Thanks!
Dan Karr

About the Author

Dan has been a CEO or Vice President for high-technology companies for the last 20 years. While working as a Senior Vice President of Marketing and Sales for a Silicon Valley company, Dan was seriously injured while commuting to work on a bicycle. After dealing with trying to get insurance companies to pay his significant medical bills, or to settle a claim so Dan could pay the medical bills, he became intimately aware of both the serious dysfunction of the insurance industry, as well as the complexity of insurance claims and lawsuits.

Knowing that the complexity of fighting claims has the effect of intimidating consumers who are victims of insurance companies, Dan decided to apply his technology marketing and sales experience to the benefit of insurance consumers. Just like consumers of technology, consumers of insurance need easy-to-understand, complete guides to what they own, how it works and what to do when it doesn't work.

Dan now lives in New Hampshire with his family. Dan's vocation is as a marketing and sales consultant to technology companies. His avocation is as a writer and advocate for owners of insurance.

You can follow Dan at:

- Facebook
- Twitter
- LinkedIn
- YouTube
- Google+

If you want an automatic email when Dan's next book is released, go to www.injuredmoney.com and navigate to the Contact page. On that page you can submit a form asking to be notified when the next book is released. Your email address will never be shared and you can unsubscribe at any time.

Word-of-mouth is crucial for any author to succeed. If you found this book useful, please remember to leave a review at your favorite retailer. Even if it's only a line or two, it would be very much appreciated.

Dan shares insight on the automobile, homeowner and health insurance industry in his blog Injured Money, which can be found at www.injuredmoney.com. He would like it if you would drop by and share your thoughts, stories and insights on the industry.

Acknowledgements

Recovering from an accident and writing a book have some striking similarities. The similarities are that both require extreme amounts of support, patience and love from those close to you. I consider myself exceptionally fortunate to be blessed with a wonderful wife, Kelly, and two sisters, Sharon and Kathryn, who continuously offer me vast amounts of support, patience and love. Their unconditional support, patience and love helped me through recovering from the accident, writing this book and in countless other ways.

Appendix A – Protect Yourself Before an Accident Occurs

Take the following easy steps before an accident occurs. Taking these steps now will help ensure you have a fair and reasonable recovery following an accident:

- Go to the following websites to get independent opinions of which companies are the best and worst at insuring their policyholders:

  - The Injured Money Rating System identifies how to measure whether an insurance company is good about paying claims. The system is based on published financial information from insurance companies. Companies rated ☆☆☆☆☆ or ☆☆☆☆☆ are the best in paying policyholders' claims. Fewer stars means the company is either not efficient at providing insurance or is keeping the premium dollars you pay in order to increase their profits. The Injured Money website will be providing a service based on this rating system so you can find out how good your insurance company is at paying claims.

  - The American Association for Justice researched and published a whitepaper identifying the Ten Worst Insurance Companies. Review this whitepaper by going to the website www.justice.org/, or accessing the whitepaper through www.injuredmoney.com. If your insurance company is on this list, you should seriously consider finding a new insurance company.

  - Check out the consumer reviews of insurance companies on the Injured Money website at www.injuredmoney.com and navigate to the Consumer Reviews page.

- Check the pure-loss ratio of insurance companies you purchase insurance from, or are considering purchasing from. The pure-loss ratio should be at least 0.7, or greater.

- Include Uninsured (UM) and UnderInsured Motorist (UIM) coverage in your policy. The minimum liability insurance coverage in most states is low and many drivers carry this minimum amount of insurance. The UIM coverage compensates you in the event the other driver's policy is insufficient.

- If you have assets you want to protect, consider adding an umbrella insurance policy with additional UM and UIM coverage on top of your automobile coverage.

Appendix B – Property Damage Claims when there is a Personal Injury

Property damage and personal injury claims are entirely different. Under a single insurance policy, the dollar limits for property damage and personal injury are uniquely specified. This means you can collect the full amount of your policy for property damage AND the full amount of your policy for personal injury.

Property damage claims are more straightforward than personal injury claims and can therefore be settled quickly. Most likely a property damage claim will be through a different claims process with a different claims representative, even within the same insurance company.

In an accident involving an automobile, the insurance coverage for property damage is based on the insurance carried on the vehicle that was at fault. If someone else hits you and they were at fault, their insurance covers your repairs or replacement. In this case, the deductible of your insurance does not apply and the other party's insurance covers all the costs. Because there will be an investigation required to determine who is at fault, you may want to proceed forward with repairs or replacement based on your own insurance (assuming you have collision / comprehensive coverage). If you do this, you will need to pay your deductible, but it will be reimbursed for the deductible when the insurance companies even up, assuming fault is assigned to the other driver.

If you were at fault in the accident, then your insurance covers the costs incurred (up to policy limits), but you must pay the deductible amount. In the case of something like a storm blowing a tree over on your car, there is no one to attribute fault to so your insurance company will pay the costs, but you must pay the deductible.

With any property damage claim, the insurance company will send a claims representative to assess the damage and determine the payment amount. In all cases, you should get at least two of your own quotes to make sure the amount the insurance company is willing to pay is accurate and covers your actual costs.

Often in property damage claims, insurance companies will have specific computer programs they use to build up the costs. In the case of auto-body repair, this could be specific repair shops that have preset prices with the insurance company for each item they repair.

You will need to go through these repair costs in great detail, examining every individual cost and negotiate the cost for each line item in the estimate. To do this effectively, you need an expert in the type of loss you have to help itemize the repair cost so you can negotiate on an item-by-item basis. In most situations, this expert could be the person who will do the work. If that does not yield a satisfactory result, there are public adjusters you can pay to help negotiate the settlement.

When paying a property damage claim, the insurance company will demand a signed release stating you have no additional recourse to collect money from them (in other words, you forfeit your ability to file a lawsuit to collect on this claim).

Note: Make sure this release does not address the bodily injury claim. Signing such a release, specific to the property damage claim, is fine. Do not sign a release unless you are 100% certain the release does not apply to your bodily injury claim.

Property Damage Claim Worksheet

Describe Loss

Description of property (include photos):

_____

_____

_____

_____

Cost to Repair

Repair cost estimates including name of repair shop:

_____

_____

_____

If Un-Repairable

Value at time of accident with supporting documentation:

_____

_____

_____

Appendix C – Accident Details Worksheet

Describe the Accident

Time:

_____

Location:

_____

Names of all parties involved:

_____

Names of witnesses:

_____

Describe what happened:

_____

_____

_____

_____

_____

Other information (weather, etc.)

_____

Responsible Party (1)

Name:

_____

Address:

_____

Telephone:

Work _____

Home _____

Cell _____

Auto:

Make _____

Model _____

License _____

Insurance

Company _____

Policy # _____

Describe what this person did:

_____

_____

_____

_____

_____

_____

Responsible Party (2)

Name:

_____

Address:

_____

Telephone:

Work

_____

Home

_____

Cell

_____

Auto:

Make

_____

Model

_____

License

_____

Insurance

Company

_____

Policy #

_____

Describe what this person did:

_____

_____

_____

_____

_____

_____

Witness (1)

Name:

_____

Address:

_____

Telephone:

Work

_____

Home

_____

Cell

_____

Date you spoke or met with the individual:

_____

Will they write down what they saw and sign it? Yes or No

Describe what they saw:

_____

_____

_____

_____

_____

_____

_____

_____

Signature: _____

Witness (2)

Name:

_____

Address:

_____

Telephone:

Work

_____

Home

_____

Cell

_____

Date you spoke or met with the individual:

_____

Will they write down what they saw and sign it? Yes or No

Describe what they saw:

_____

_____

_____

_____

_____

_____

_____

Signature:

Witness (3)

Name:

_____

Address:

_____

Telephone:

Work

_____

Home

_____

Cell

_____

Date you spoke or met with the individual:

_____

Will they write down what they saw and sign it? Yes or No

Describe what they saw:

_____

_____

_____

_____

_____

_____

_____

_____

Signature:

_____

Appendix D – Insurance Information

Responsible Party

Company name:

_____

Address:

_____

Telephone:

Work

_____

Home

_____

Cell

_____

Adjuster (1):

_____

Adjuster (2):

_____

Communication with Responsible Party

Who:

_____

Date:

_____

What was said:

_____

_____

_____

Action items:

_____

_____

Communication with Responsible Party

Who:

_____

Date:

_____

What was said:

_____

_____

Action items:

_____

_____

Communication with Responsible Party

Who:

_____

Date:

_____

What was said:

_____

_____

_____

Action items:

_____

_____

Communication with Responsible Party

Who:

_____

Date:

_____

What was said:

_____

_____

Action items:

_____

_____

Other Involved Party

Company name:

_____

Address:

_____

Telephone:

  Work

_____

  Fax

_____

  Cell

_____

Adjuster (1):

_____

Adjuster (2):

_____

Communication with Other Involved Party

Who:

_____

Date:

_____

What was said:

_____

_____

Action items:

_____

Communication with Other Involved Party

Who:

_____

Date:

_____

What was said:

_____

_____

Action items:

_____

_____

Communication with Other Involved Party

Who:

_____

Date:

_____

What was said:

_____

_____

Action items:

_____

_____

Communication with Other Involved Party

Who:

_____

Date:

_____

What was said:

_____

_____

Action items:

_____

_____

Communication with Other Involved Party

Who:

_____

Date:

_____

What was said:

_____

_____

Action items:

_____

_____

Appendix E – Medical Bills

The table below shows how to keep track of your medical bills. Following the table is a description of what each column means.

	Invoice Amount	Insurance Paid Amount	Deductible Amount	Description	Service Date	Hospital / Dr. Name
	$1,500.00	$900.00	$100.00	Ambulance	Jan. 2	Ambulance Co.
	$100.00	$60.00	$10.00	X-ray	Jan. 2	Hosp. XYZ
	$2,500.00	$1,500.00	$250.00	Emerg. Rm	Jan. 2	Hosp. XYZ
	$8,000.00	$4,500.00	$400.00	Surgery	Jan. 3	Dr. QRS
	$5,500.00	$3,000.00	$255.00	Hospital	Jan. 3	Hosp. XYZ
	$1,250.00	$650.00	$100.00	Anesthesiologist	Jan. 3	Dr. BZD
	$100.00	$60.00	$10.00	X-ray	Jan. 3	Hosp. XYZ
	$475.00	$200.00	$100.00	Med. Supplies	Jan. 3	Hosp. XYZ
	$1,200.00	$600.00	$60.00	Therapy	Jan. 5	Clinic QRS
Total	$20,625.00	$11,470.00	$1,285.00			

Invoice Amount: This is one of the two most important columns in the spreadsheet. In this column you include the invoice amounts of each medical bill you receive. The total in this column is what you use to calculate pain and suffering.

> *Note*: If you were seen by multiple doctors for a single injury and they had differing opinions, only provide the name, reports, invoices and dollar amounts for the doctor who ultimately treated you. The conflicting information between two doctors can and will be used against you.

Insurance Paid Amount: This is the other of the two most important columns in the spreadsheet. In this column you list what the insurance company actually paid each doctor, hospital or other medical provider. The way the system works is that the doctor or hospital invoices a certain amount, but the medical insurance company pays a reduced rate that they previously negotiated. Thus, if you look in the first row, you will see that a doctor billed $1,500 for a certain procedure but the insurance company only really paid $900 of this $1,500 bill. This paid invoice amount is very important because if you have to pay back your medical insurance after you receive a claim, you only need to pay them back this smaller amount that they paid and not the full invoice amount.

Deductible Amount: This column totals your out-of-pocket expenses.

Description, Service Date, Hospital / Dr. Name: These descriptions are all there for the same two reasons: First, so you can easily review the list for completeness, and second, at some point following an accident where there are significant medical bills, questions are going to come up such as a doctor didn't get paid or an invoice is wrong. These columns will enable you to easily reference everything about your medical records, and to categorize them by injury.

Appendix F – Statute of Limitations & Small Claims Limit by State

State	Statute of Limitations (years)	Small Claims Court Dollar ($) Limit
Alabama	2	$3,000
Alaska	2	$10,000
Arizona	2	$2,500
Arkansas	3	$5,000
California	2	$7,500
Colorado	2	$7,500
Connecticut	2	$5,000
Delaware	2	$5,000
District of Columbia	3	$15,000
Florida	4	$5,000
Georgia	2	$15,000
Hawaii	2	$3,500
Idaho	2	$5,000
Illinois	2	$10,000
Indiana	2	$6,000
Iowa	2	$5,000
Kansas	2	$4,000
Kentucky	1	$1,500
Louisiana	1	$3,000
Maine	6	$6,000
Maryland	3	$5,000
Massachusetts	3	$7,000
Michigan	3	$3,000
Minnesota	2	$7,500
Mississippi	3	$3,500
Missouri	5	$3,000

State	Statute of Limitations (years)	Small Claims Court Dollar ($) Limit
Montana	3	$3,000
Nebraska	4	$5,000
Nevada	2	$5,000
New Hampshire	3	$7,500
New Mexico	3	$1,000
New York	3	$5,000
North Carolina	3	$5,000
North Dakota	6	$1,000
Ohio	2	$3,000
Oklahoma	2	$6,000
Oregon	2	$7,500
Pennsylvania	2	$8,000
Rhode Island	3	$2,500
South Carolina	3	$7,500
South Dakota	3	$12,000
Tennessee	1	$25,000
Texas	2	$10,000
Utah	4	$10,000
Vermont	3	$50,000
Virginia	2	$5,000
Washington	3	$5,000
West Virginia	2	$5,000
Wisconsin	3	$5,000
Wyoming	4	$5,000

Glossary of Terms

Arbitration: A process where a mutually agreed to, independent, arbitrator presides over a hearing and makes a decision on the issue being decided. The arbitrator's decision is typically binding with no option for appeal.

Award: To be given something that is due or merited by decree or order.

Bad Faith: The improper denial of insurance claims. An example of bad faith would be delaying or denying claims without a legitimate reason.

Contingency Fee: A fee agreement characterized by "no win, no fee."

Damages: The money equivalent for property damage or injuries sustained.

Demand Letter: The letter sent to an insurance company when an insurance claim is filed. This letter states the demands of the person filing the claim.

Depose: To testify under oath.

Deposition: The act of being deposed, or examine, under oath.

Fault: Responsible for the accident.

Fraud: To trick or deceive for the purpose of gaining a profit.

Liability: Moneys owed, debt.

Liability Insurance: Protects the purchaser from liabilities resulting from lawsuits.

Mediation: A process where a third party facilitates reconciliation. The process is not binding; leaving both parties with the option of rejecting the proposed solutions and proceeding forward with a trial by jury.

Medical Lien: A legal claim by a medical insurance company on money paid by an auto insurer to reimburse the costs of providing medical care necessary as a result of the accident.

Medical Special Damages: The total amount of medical bills.

Negligent: Careless.

Personal Injury: An injury to the body, mind or emotions.

Policy Limit: The maximum amount payable as defined by the insurance policy.

Property Damage: The destruction of property such as automobile or home.

Punitive Damages: Damages awarded with the intent to serve as punishment to the guilty party. An example of when punitive damages may be awarded is a case where the guilty party intentionally hurt the victim.

Reimbursement: Repayment of a financial obligation.

Statute of Limitations: The maximum time during which legal action can be taken following an event.

Treble Damages: A tripling of the damages due.

UnderInsured Motorist (UIM) Coverage: Insurance you purchase for your own benefit covering yourself, your passengers and your vehicle in the event of an accident and the responsible party does not have enough liability coverage to pay the damages.

Uninsured Motorist (UM) Coverage: Provides insurance to the purchaser in the event of an accident and the responsible party does not have liability coverage to pay the damages.

Umbrella Policy: Liability insurance in excess of the coverage other policies (such as auto) contain.

End Notes

[1] Property/Casualty Insurance in 2008: *Overpriced Insurance and Underpaid Claims Result in Unjustified Profits, Padded Reserves and Excessive Capitalization* (Consumer Federation of America publication, 2008)

[2] Feinman, Jay M., *Delay, Deny, Defend: Why Insurance Companies Don't Pay Claims and What You Can Do About It* (New York, Penguin, 2010), 76

[3] Feinman, Jay M., *Delay, Deny, Defend: Why Insurance Companies Don't Pay Claims and What You Can Do About It* (New York, Penguin, 2010), 74

[4] Feinman, Jay M., *Delay, Deny, Defend: Why Insurance Companies Don't Pay Claims and What You Can Do About It* (New York, Penguin, 2010), 75 - 76, 88

[5] Feinman, Jay M., *Delay, Deny, Defend: Why Insurance Companies Don't Pay Claims and What You Can Do About It* (New York, Penguin, 2010), 79

[6] Feinman, Jay M., *Delay, Deny, Defend: Why Insurance Companies Don't Pay Claims and What You Can Do About It* (New York, Penguin, 2010), 79

[7] Feinman, Jay M., *Delay, Deny, Defend: Why Insurance Companies Don't Pay Claims and What You Can Do About It* (New York, Penguin, 2010), 84

[8] Feinman, Jay M., *Delay, Deny, Defend: Why Insurance Companies Don't Pay Claims and What You Can Do About It* (New York, Penguin, 2010), 30

[9] Berardinelli, Freeman and Shaw, *From Good Hands to Boxing Gloves – How Allstate Changed Casualty Insurance in America* (Trial Guides, 2006), 131,133, 135

[10] Hunter, J. Robert, Property/Casualty Insurance in 2008: *Overpriced Insurance and Underpaid Claims Result in Unjustified Profits, Padded Reserves and Excessive Capitalization* (2008), 22

CPSIA information can be obtained at www.ICGtesting.com
Printed in the USA
LVOW05s1619150814

399349LV00017B/1152/P